The moving finger writes,
and having writ

Moves on; nor all your
piety nor wit

Shall lure it back to cancel
half a line

Nor all your tears wash
out a word of it.

Stanza 71
The Rubaiyat of
Omar Khayyam

*Issued under the direction of the Council of
Women for Home Missions*

IN RED MAN'S LAND

A Study of The American Indian

BY

FRANCIS E. LEUPP

Former United States Commissioner of Indian Affairs
Author of
" The Indian and His Problem "

Illustrated

GLORIETA, NEW MEXICO · 87535

© 1976
The Rio Grande Press, Inc.,
Glorieta, NM 87535

First edition from which this edition was
reproduced was supplied by
T. N. LUTHER, Books,
P. O. Box 6083
Shawnee Mission, Ks. 66206

Photographically enlarged in reproduction

Library of Congress Cataloging in Publication Data

Leupp, Francis Ellington, 1849-1918.
   In red man's land.

   Reprint of the ed. published by F. H. Revell Co.,
New York, issued in series: Interdenominational
home mission study course; with new pref. and introd.
   Bibliography: p.
   1. Indians of North America. 2. Indians of
North America--Missions. I. Title. II. Series:
Interdenominational home mission study course.
E77.L64   1976   970'.004'97   76-44529
ISBN 0-87380-115-6

A RIO GRANDE CLASSIC
First published in 1914

First Printing 1976

The Rio Grande Press, Inc.

GLORIETA, NEW MEXICO · 87535

Publisher's Preface

This is not a very big book, as dimensions and size goes, but it is otherwise a *great big book;* it is, moreover, a *good* book. It is not very timely in one sense, having been written in 1913 and published in 1914—sixty two years ago, but what author Francis Ellington Leupp has set forth here is a testimony to the fact that ever since the Whiteman first confronted the Redman in the New World, there have been men (of both races) who *tried* each to understand the other. Author Leupp writes with a passion bordering on inspiration. His words are cogent and eloquent, his writing lucid and graceful. His innate compassion is evident on every page. His grasp of the difficulty in establishing and maintaining a racially pluralistic social order is profound.

So we chose this small volume as one of our beautiful Rio Grande Classics—because of what this one Whiteman has written. Even as all Redmen are not alike, neither are all Whitemen. Leupp is not the only Whiteman to take up verbal cudgels on behalf of the First Americans. There are many, many others—far too many to attempt to list in these few pages here. For instance (we will mention one, for obvious reasons): in 1832, eighty two years before Leupp's work, author Benjamin B. Thatcher wrote a similar two-volume study entitled Indian Biography, or, *An Historical Account of Those Individuals Who Have Been Distinguished Among the North American Natives as Orators, Warriors, Statesmen and Other Remarkable Characters,* a title which speaks for itself and which we reprinted in 1973. There were others before Thatcher, all the way back to Roger Williams (1603-1683).

A great many Whitemen have devoted their lives to Christian ideals, one of which consists of bringing Christianity to the aborigine wherever he might be found. In the eyes of most of these well-intentioned people (long gone, and contemporary), Christianity and civilization were (are) synonymous, i.e., if the aborigine could be Christianized, he would automatically be "civilized". The idea prevalent today that the Whiteman has always and universally been the "enemy" of the aborigine in general, and the Redman in particular, is preposterous; the mortal conflicts that arose in America with ever-increasing ferocity were most often tit-for-tat provocations by one side or the other.

Early on, Whitemen coming from Europe to the New World were aghast at the idea of a *continent* inhabited for—who knew?—thousands of years but which had produced nothing equatable with the social, economic and political order of the Old World. As the Whiteman pushed forward, ever west, and the Redman retreated before him, a veritable host of the "invaders" tried to impress (or impose?) the Christian ethos upon the unwilling and uncomprehending Redman. The Whiteman was motivated thus by his own milieu—Christianity meant civilization; civilization meant Christianity. It was un-Christian of the Whiteman, in the eyes of most of them, to know the pleasures and comforts of civilization while the Redman—the Whiteman's neighbor—did not. Indeed, did not the Good Book *require* the Christian to *love* his neighbor?

So here at The Rio Grande Press we thought it appropriate to present once again this fine book, timely in intent if not in chronology. We particularly urge our Redman cousins to ponder the notion that author Leupp so often stresses—friendliness with Whiteman is most apt and often to breed friendliness in return; provocation breeds provocation. While inter-racial love may not necessarily breed love, inter-racial hate absolutely breeds hate.

The first edition from which this edition was reproduced was supplied by our friend T. N. Luther, Books, of Shawnee Mission, Kansas. "Tal", as he is known to his many friends everywhere, is one of the best in the rare book business, a gentleman, and, of course, a scholar.

As we have standardized our beautiful Rio Grande Classics on two sizes only, this edition has been photographically enlarged in reproduction. The dimensions of the first edition made it practically a pocket-size book; it was 4 7/8 inches wide, 7 1/2 inches high. Our edition is 6 inches by 9 inches. The enlargement process increases the typesize and improves the halftone cuts, making it easier to read and look at, but alas! it also enlarges such imperfections of the original printing as are there, and not noticeable in the first edition format.

It has been our custom now for years to place into our editions new emendatory material germane to the subject, such as photographs, maps, charts, indexes, words like these, and introductions from erudite and eminent scholars. We felt that this title was written in such a way that an index could not be prepared, so there is none now and there was none in the first edition. However, we *could* add an introduction by a scholar in the field, and we did. We asked our friend Associate Professor Theodore (Ted) R. Frisbie, Ph.D., of the anthropology department of Southern Illinois University at Edwardsville, to write something for us. His words follow ours. We appreciate his excellent research, and we extend him our *kudos* and thanks for a very fine piece of work.

We suppose we should mention the poem inscribed so prettily on the very first page of this edition; it was not in the original copy. It serves a purpose, we believe. The author of the poem, who lived some 900 years ago, was one of the many educated sons of an Arabian tentmaker grown wealthy in his craft. The lad's name was Omar Khayyam. As a youth—a very prescient and perceptive young man, obviously—he wrote a *Rubaiyat* around a litany of aphorisms. This one—the 71st stanza of his *opus magnum*—offers an immutable truth, one of the eternal verities so besought by the ancient Greek philosphers. We thought the reader of this book should take note of this nugget of knowledge, so we have inserted it herewithin our edition. Ponder it well, reader.

This is the 112th beautiful Rio Grande Classic; we are pleased that we can make it available once again after so many years of idleness in a bibliographic limbo. It is *worth* reading, and we urge you to read it.

Robert B. McCoy

La Casa Escuela
Glorieta, NM 87535
September 1975

Introduction

The fascination that surrounds learning something new is an ever present phenomenon among the human species; perhaps it is the very reason why we have progressed as far as we have. The printed word embodies the essence of knowledge, particularly when these words are arranged to form a book which has something worthwhile to say. The present volume, *In Red Man's Land,* is of this caliber. Although contemporary anthropologists would reject the use of a unilinear evolutionary framework for ordering discussions of Indians and undoubtedly would question the meaning of phrases such as "marriage by purchase," such schemes and terminological usages were typical of 1914, the time when the volume was written. If one can accept these as such, one discovers that the volume speaks eloquently for itself.

Precisely who was Francis E. Leupp?[1] The title page tells readers that he was "Former United States Commissioner of Indian Affairs (and the) Author of *The Indian and His Problem.*" There is, of course, much more to be said on his behalf. Francis Ellington Leupp was born in New York, New York on January 2, 1849. He attended Williams College and graduated at the age of 21 in 1870. A consuming interest in journalism led to his employment by the *New York Evening Post* where he served as assistant editor. During

1878, he bought an interest in the *Syracuse Herald* and became its editor. Syracuse, New York, however, did not offer much of a political challenge to the newspaperman; and Leupp began spending some of his time in the nation's capital. In 1885 he began contributing articles to the *New York Evening Post* from Washington, and in 1889, he became the paper's official Washington correspondent, a position he held for fifteen years. During this same period Leupp served as editor of *Good Government,* the official publication of the National Civil Service Reform League. His activities and efforts on behalf of the League were of the kind that enable us to view him as a pioneer leader in such reform. (New York Times 1918)

Equally important, and in many ways related were Leupp's ideas concerning "common sense" treatment of the American Indians. Official involvement with Indians and their problems began while Leupp was a member of the United States Board of Indian Commissioners, from 1862 to 1895. Following this, it was not until 1903 that Leupp was again called into official service. At that time, President Theodore Roosevelt was looking for an individual to investigate alleged wrongdoings by officers at the Kiowa Indian Agency at Anadarko, Oklahoma. The person chosen for the job had to be knowledgeable about Indian affairs, but not connected with the government; Francis Leupp was the logical choice. Leupp was appointed a special supervisor of education and began his work in June, 1903. In July, he went to Anadarko to conduct the inquiry. Upon returning to Washington, he wrote an extensive report exonerating the officers at the Agency. The report was submitted to the Secretary of the Interior who, in turn presented it to the Senate for publication on December 15, 1903 (Leupp 1903). The thoroughness of Leupp's research is astounding, even today. The report includes a statement of each allegation, presentation of all of Leupp's related findings, and thoughtful evaluations of all the data; there is no doubt that the job was well done.

Within a year after the completion of the Kiowa Agency report, the following appeared in the *Journal of the Executive Proceedings of the Senate* (1931: 346)

White House, December 6, 1904
To the Senate of the United States:

I nominate Francis E. Leupp, of the District of Columbia, to be Commissioner of Indian Affairs, vice William A. Jones resigned.

Theodore Roosevelt

The next day Leupp was appointed: he served as Commissioner of Indian Affairs from 1905 to 1909.

The events, problems and decisions of each year of his tenure is the office of Commissioner are presented in annual reports to the Secretary of the Interior. While some of the data contained in these reports are alluded to in the present volume, the full scope of Leupp's understanding of the American Indians and his thoughts about what should be done to enable them to enter the mainstream of American life while preserving aspects of their own cultures are to be found in the yearly reports (Leupp 1905, 1906, 1907 and 1909). Frequently Leupp's personal thoughts occur as digressions. For example, the following is typical: "While on this subject, I trust I may be pardoned if I volunteer a few thoughts as to the policy to be pursued . . ." (Leupp 1906:36).

Leupp's goals, as Commissioner of Indian Affairs, included those of providing education for the Indians, developing ways by which they could make sufficient livelihoods through employment and ultimately, removing the American Indians from the rolls as government wards. Examples of his approach are numerous, and worthy of consideration:

(From *Stopping One Source of Waste*)

As you are aware, I have been making for the last three years rather extended tours of the Indian country, aiming as far as possible to visit agencies and schools which have never been visited by a Commissioner before, and which rarely get a visit from anyone representing directly the Washington administration. Among other valuable fruits of these visitations has been the opportunity to observe what stocks of unused but usable material are on hand in the several storehouses, not capable of being applied to local needs and yet too good for condemnation. Here and there at other places I find serious lacks in equipment. A year ago I made a systematic effort to obtain accurate statistics as to both lacks and over-supplies, which would enable me very often to avoid the expense of a purchase to meet some deficiency, by simply transferring material from one place where it is not wanted to another place where it is (Leupp 1907:11-12)

. . . .

(From *A Beet Farming Project)*

Now, suppose that the Indian, instead of having to take his chances with tenants of this sort, could rent three, four or five hundred acres of his family's lands in excess of what he is competent to till himself, to a company with large capital who has set up within a few miles of his home a factory for converting his crops into a commercial staple which is always in demand at good prices. Suppose that the company not only pays him rent, but improves and extends his irrigating facilities; puts his soil into rich condition and keeps it so by intensive farming; employs experts to show him how to do the same thing with his 20 acres that it is doing with the surplus; buys of him what he raises himself; hires at good day wages any members of his family who can be spared from the necessary work on their little homestead; remains in possession for twenty or twenty-five years, and thus saves the need of finding a new tenant at the end of each five; and finally, when its occupancy ends, turns back in improved land, buildings, fences, irrigation extensions, etc., a vastly more valuable piece of property than it took over: can anyone question that he is permanently better off, and better equipped for the rest of his struggle for a livelihood?

. . . .

What makes the capitalist invest in the corporation is the desire to make his accumulated wealth earn him more of the comforts and luxuries of life; what the corporation works for is to keep itself alive by satisfying the investor; what the boss works for is to support himself and his dependents by satisfying the corporation that employs him, and what the laborer works for is to keep himself and his family fed and clad by satisfying the boss. That is where the Indian comes in when he is the laborer; and not all the governmental supervision, and all the schools, and all the philanthropic activities set afoot in his behalf by benevolent whites, if rolled into one and continued for a century, would begin to compare in educational value and efficiency with ten years of work under bosses whose own bread and butter depend upon their making him a success as a small farmer.

What astonishes me is the indifference of some of our lawmakers toward the project I have outlined here in its obvious relation to the upbuilding of the frontier country—the same great West for which the Congress has usually so kind a side. That very fact, however, spurs my courage to keep up the agitation in the face of obstacles; for I am bound to believe that the members who now regard it askance have not yet fully grasped its secondary significance. The proposition is not simply one for the benefit of the Indians, but quite as much for the upbuilding of the States concerned. (Leupp 1906:9-10, 11).

. . . .

(From *Indian Labor Outside of Reservations*)

. . . In my last annual report I spoke of an undertaking upon which the Office and just entered in the Southwest, the maintenance of an employment bureau for finding Indians who want to work and finding the work for the Indians who want it. This bureau has been in the care of Charles F. Dagenett, in whose veins is a strain of Indian blood, and whose efforts are therefore sympathetic as well as practical. The results of the first year's experiment have been most encouraging. During the last season some six hundred Indians, including both adults and schoolboys, have found employment in the open labor market as railroad construction laborers, irrigation-ditch diggers, beet farmers, and in other occupations. (Leupp 1906:12).

. . . .

(From *Education*)

I take special pleasure in reporting a net increase of six in the number of day schools maintained among the Indians, for these little schools not only perform the usual functions of such institutions with the pupils themselves, but radiate knowledge of better habits of life and a higher morality thru the tepees, cabins, and camps to which the children return every night. They are, in my judgment, the greatest general civilizing agency of any thru which we try to operate upon the rising generation (Leupp 1906:50)

—

. . . .

(From *Institutes*)

The purpose of holding several institutes [for teachers] each year is to bring the system of Indian education to a higher standard of efficiency. In different localities are found different types of Indians and varying conditions, and by comparison of methods and interchange of ideas each teacher present and each school represented receives the benefit of the experience of the others. Thus the local institutes are as valuable in their way as the general institutes, and are attended by many who would otherwise be deprived of any institute opportunities (Leupp 1906:75).

. . . .

(From *Thumb-Print Signatures*)

Beginning in 1905, I adopted the practice of requiring, as evidence of the authenticity of written agreements with Indians, the thumb prints of the signers in addition to their signatures. It has worked so well that it will be continued as a regular feature in all negotiations of importance (Leupp 1907:14).

On the basis of all that had been accomplished and dreamed while serving as Commissioner of Indian Affairs, Francis Leupp wrote his first book, *The Indian and His Problem, (New York, 1910);* immediately after completing his service. In it he sought to present an overall picture of American Indian relations with the United States Government while emphasizing what should be done to assist the Indians in achieving a way of life congruent with mainstream American culture. Four years later, the present companion volume appeared. While it attempts to present a more individualistic view of the American Indians, there are, as one would expect, some overall similarities.

It is interesting to note in the present volume that data pertaining to treaties (see Chapter 2) and land grabbing are presented in a straightforward manner. Although not cited, even George Washington was not above attempting to secure rich lands *against* royal decree as the colonists pushed westward beyond the Appalachians. In a letter written to his friend, William Crawford, on September 21, 1767, Washington suggested how restrictions relating to size might be evaded. He emphasized that he would like very much

> . . . to join you in attempting to secure some of the most valuable Lands in the King's part which I think may be accomplished after a while not withstanding the Proclamation that restrains it at present and prohibits the Settling of them at all for I can never look upon that Proclamation in any other light (but this I say between ourselves) than as a temporary expedient to quiet the Minds of the Indians . . . (Fitzpatrick 1931:II: 468)

For Francis Leupp, however, land grabbing was but one of the many unfair practices carried out against the American Indians. Through compassion and deeds, he sought to correct the wrongs as he saw them, and thus, pave the way for a better way of life for Native Americans. His death on November 19, 1918 at his home at Stoneleigh Court, Washington, D.C., preceded the Meriam Report (Meriam and Associates 1928) by a decade. In many ways, Leupp's ideas foreshadowed the new policy, especially in the emphasis on Indians achieveing equality with whites through education, economic and health improvement programs. The primary difference lay in Leupp's support of a policy of assimilation, and the Meriam Report's emphasis on cultural pluralism. The new philosophy as well as its implementation may be largely credited to John Collier, who slightly later served as Commissioner of Indian Affairs (1933-1945). Unfortunately, following Collier's retirement, the approach was not continued; however, the 1970s have seen a modified version take effect, one which is midway between the assimilationist and cultural pluralist stances.

Having briefly reviewed some of the data relevant to understanding Leupp and his contributions, as well as touching upon more recent occurences, I should like to conclude by referring the reader to two recent publications: *A History of Indian Policy* (Tyler 1973) and *The Ethnics in American Politics: American Indians* (Svensson 1973). Each of these offers a more complete description and discussion of the Bureau of Indian Affairs.

Theodore R. Frisbie
Associate Professor of Anthropology

Southern Illinois University
Edwardsville, Illinois
August, 1976

References Cited

Fitzpatrick, John (ed).
    1931   The Writings of George Washington II. Washington, D.C.: United States Government Printing Office.

Leupp, Francis E.

    1903   The Results of an Investigation into the Affairs of the Kiowa Indian Agency. Washington, D.C.: Senate Documents, 58th Congress, Second Session. Document 26.

    1905   Report of the Commissioner of Indian Affairs to the Secretary of the Interior, 1905. Washington, D.C.: Government Printing Office.

    1906   Report of the Commissioner of Indian Affairs to the Secretary of the Interior, 1906. Washington, D.C.: Government Printing Office.

    1907   Report of the Commissioner of Indian Affairs to the Secretary of the Interior, 1907. Washington, D.C.: Government Printing Office.

    1909   Report of the Commissioner of Indian Affairs to the Secretary of the Interior, 1908. Washington, D.C.: Government Printing Office.

    1910   The Indian and His Problem. New York: Scribner and Sons.

Meriam, Lewis and Associates

1928   The Problem of Indian Administration. Baltimore:
        Johns Hopkins Press.

New York Times

1918   Obituary of Francis E. Leupp. November 20; page 15,
        column 4.

Svensson, Frances

1973   The Ethnics in American Politics: American Indians.
        Minneapolis: Burgess Publishing Company.

Tyler, S. Lyman

1973   A History of Indian Policy. Washington, D.C.: United
        States Department of the Interior, Bureau of Indian
        Affairs.

United States Senate

1931   Journal of the Executive Proceedings of the Senate of
        the United States of America. 58th Congress, First,
        Second and Third Sessions (November 9, 1903-
        March 3, 1905), Volume 35. Washington, D.C.:
        Government Printing Office.

Van Valkenburgh. Richard F.

1941   Diné Bikéyah (The Navajos Country). Window Rock: United States Department of the Interior, Office of Indian Affairs, Navajo Service. (Edited by L. Adams and J. McPhee).

Theodore R. Frisbie

NOTE

[1]As a surname, Leupp is not common. The only Leupp I could recall was Leupp, Arizona, located a short distance northwest of Winslow. Since this is the location of a jurisdictional agency on the Navajo Reservation, and the site of both a boarding school and hospital, I thought there might be a connection. In point of fact, there is. The Bureau of Indian Affairs settlement was established in 1908 and named in Leupp's honor. (Van ValKenburgh 1941:87).

PRESENT DAY WARRIORS.

*Issued under the direction of the Council of
Women for Home Missions*

IN RED MAN'S LAND

A Study of The American Indian

BY

FRANCIS E. LEUPP

Former United States Commissioner of Indian Affairs
Author of
" The Indian and His Problem "

Illustrated

NEW YORK   CHICAGO   TORONTO

Fleming H. Revell Company

LONDON   AND   EDINBURGH

New York: 158 Fifth Avenue
Chicago: 125 N. Wabash Ave.
Toronto: 25 Richmond St., W.
London: 21 Paternoster Square
Edinburgh: 100 Princes Street

AUTHOR'S PREFACE

IN the pages which follow I have tried to avoid going over any of the ground covered by " The Indian and His Problem." The purpose of that work was to set forth the larger relations of the aboriginal race to our governmental mechanism, and to indicate the lines of legislation and administration necessary to their proper adjustment. In " In Red Man's Land " my aim has been to deal with the Indian as an individual, as if I were introducing an old resident to new neighbors. As the two books present respectively the civic and the human aspects of the Indian, they are designed to supplement each other wherever they appeal to the same readers. The generous reception accorded my earlier volume encourages me to hope for equal consideration for its successor.

F. E. L.

WASHINGTON, D. C.,

CONTENTS

ILLUSTRATIONS

I

THE ABORIGINAL RED MAN

Long ago the Great Mystery caused this land to be, and made the Indians to live in this land. Well has the Indian fulfilled all the intent of the Great Mystery for him.

The white man has never known the Indian. It is thus: there are two roads, the white man's road and the Indian's road. Neither traveler knows the road of the other. Thus ever has it been, from the long-ago even unto to-day.

I want all Indians and white men to read and learn how the Indians lived and thought in the olden time, and may it bring holy-good upon the younger Indians to know of their fathers. A little while and the old Indians will no longer be, and the young will be even as white men.—CHIEF HIAMOVI, in "The Indian's Book."

> As monumental bronze unchanged his look:
> A soul that pity touched, but never shook:
> Trained, from his tree-rocked cradle to his bier,
> The fierce extremes of good and ill to brook
> Impassive—fearing but the shame of fear—
> A stoic of the woods—a man without a tear.
>   —CAMPBELL.

I

THE ABORIGINAL RED MAN

PERSONS who know how much I have been in Red Man's Land sometimes remark, in entire sincerity: "Of course, you understand the Indian language?" They are astonished when told that there is no "Indian language"; that between fifty and sixty distinct tongues exist among the Indians in the United States, and that every one of these has sundry dialects, so that it would be safe to say that two or three hundred languages are spoken by as many groups of our Indian neighbors. As the Indians now living number roughly three hundred thousand, this would average one language to, say, every twelve hundred. Actually, there is nothing like so even a division. There are several remnants of tribes to-day which contain less than one hundred souls. Indeed, a few years ago an Indian was discovered who was absolutely, as far as could be ascertained, the sole survivor of his people.

Out of the primitive Babel was developed, in one part of our country, a language of signs. In the old days, when the bison ranged over the mid-continental plains, hunting parties of Indians from different tribes would occasionally meet in a common chase. Neither in asking nor in giving information orally could one

party understand the other; so resort was had to
various motions of the head, hands, fingers, arms and
body which would convey an idea by suggestion, like
spreading downward the first and second fingers of
one hand, bestriding with them the outstretched fore-
finger of the other, and moving the combination forward with short vertical curves to indicate a man rid-
ing a horse. Many years of use elaborated the system
from a few signs with obvious meanings to a multitude whose relation to the main source was more or
less remote. Even to-day, among the older members
of the plains tribes, are several thorough masters of
the art of sign-communication, and I have seen some
of them converse for hours without uttering an audi-
ble word.

I mention the diversity of languages among the
Indians because it typifies their diversities generally,
and illustrates the difficulty of writing about the characteristics of a race broken into groups which differ as
widely as corresponding groups of our own race. In
whatever follows, therefore, the reader must bear in
mind that I am not attempting to depict the life and
traits of all the Indians on the one hand, or of any
particular tribe on the other. Rather, I am trying
to give him a composite impression, in very limited
space, of a subject broad in scope and embarrassing
in detail. For the purpose of this chapter, moreover,
I must confine my attention to the Indian as he was
before he had passed under Caucasian influence. Of
the more modern type I shall speak later.

At the very outset of his life, the Indian of yore
was sure of warm welcome. His people had not

learned to regard a family as a burden. The simple habits of the Indian woman raised no obstacles to her giving birth to a babe to-day and resuming her round of life to-morrow at the latest. She had never bound her body in stiff sheaths. She could stir about her daily work, or tramp for many miles when moving camp, without exhaustion, because she used the whole sole of her foot in walking, and her gait was steadied by long practice in carrying an open water-vessel on her head. She spent most of her time in the fresh air and sunlight. The muscles of her chest and arms, hips and back, were strengthened by burden-bearing, and kept mobile by wielding the rude implements with which she dressed big game or cultivated her patch of corn and beans. In spite of the harm occasionally wrought by overdoing, there is no doubt that the regimen of nomadic camp life better fitted a woman for bearing and rearing a family than the artificialities of our highly organized society.

The father welcomed the baby as heartily as the mother. He loved children for their own sake. Their pranks and prattle entertained him, and he was undisturbed by forebodings for their future. He had not spent a lifetime at hard delving, and grasping at hazards that turned his hair prematurely gray, in order to amass a fortune on whose income his progeny could live in idleness. Sufficient unto the day, was the rule for him. If, before the snows came, he had stored up enough dry food to tide him over those periods when the drifts forbade hunting, he settled down into his winter quarters with a contented heart. With the dawn of spring he was off at once for the woods and streams, or to wage a war of plunder upon some enemy. If his stores had given out meanwhile, there might be neighbors more fortunate; and food was one of the necessaries every one was presumed to be willing to share with a friend in distress.

This was the little world into which the babe was ushered—one that was ready for it in a simple, unstudied way, and that counted it an asset rather than an added liability. It is true that a son's greeting may have been a trifle more demonstrative than a daughter's, but even a daughter was not unwelcome. Though she could be of no direct value in war or the chase, she could be trained to cook and care for the camp; and the chances were that, when she attained a marriageable age, she would be sought as a wife by some man who, in the ardor of his courtship, would be willing to present her parents with dried foods, hides or blankets, pipes or tobacco, in quantities sufficient to compensate them for the loss of her companionship.

No skilled surgeons or white-capped nurses were at the mother's bedside when the little one came. Some older woman of the camp was there, perhaps, to lend a hand in case of need, and the father to note the omens. Over the hill yonder a vagrant coyote might be peering toward the tepee in which the new life was beginning. Possibly it was very early in the morning, and the coyote bayed at the moon which had not yet faded from the heavens. Here was an omen which the father was quick to seize upon: the child, born just as the coyote's open mouth was lifted upward, should bear for its infant name, "Laughs-at-the-Sky."

It is a fashion among whites to make fun of the eccentricities of Indian nomenclature; but perhaps, if we look underneath the surface, we find as much that is reasonable in it as in the corresponding practice among our own ancestors, who named a boy Theodore because it meant a "gift from God," or adopted the surname Smith because the head of the family was a worker in metals. A name, after all, is of value only for identification; and the Indians followed good Jewish precedent in re-naming a person at various stages of his career when he had done or suffered something worthy of such commemoration.

While Laughs-at-the-Sky remained a little child he wore no clothing, except in the coldest winter weather, when his mother would wrap him in a hide which she had tanned herself and made so soft that it folded about his body almost like cloth. Until he could walk, he spent much of his time on a baby-board, the Indian equivalent of a cradle. This was a short, thin, flat slab, with wrappings lashed to its lower end so that a baby laid upon it could be swathed and tied fast as neatly as a Caucasian infant is tucked into its more pretentious bed. The advantage of the board over a cradle was that it could be lifted and slung against the mother's back, and thus she could carry her baby about with her as she moved from place to place. When she was tired of carrying it, she could set it upright against the nearest tree or shrub, whence the baby could watch what was going on far better than if it were on its back, seeing everything at a

distorted angle. More important yet, the baby-board,
by virtue of being shaped somewhat like the human
form, kept the trunk and extremities of its little tenant continually in a normal position; and this undoubtedly went far toward giving the adult Indian, in his
primitive state, his arrow-like straightness.

Grown old enough to run about and play, Laughs-
at-the-Sky amused himself with a toy bow and arrow
made for him by his father, taking aim, as he walked
across the prairie or through the woods, at every
bird or rabbit he scared up. When his father went
to bathe in the neighboring creek, the little fellow
trotted along, and was first duly immersed, and then
left to splash in the shallow water at will. At an
early age he picked up the art of swimming, as the
small wildings learn it, partly by intuition and partly
by imitation. In this matter, as in many another
which contributed to his training for life, there was
no compulsion from his elders. He was not violently
scolded, or threatened with a whipping, or sent to
bed without his supper for naughtiness. There was
no effort to break his will, or discipline him to the
point where obedience degenerates into subservience.
His father and mother left him very much to himself, even their occasional admonitions being delivered
with no evidence of strong feeling. The whole atmosphere of the camp was temperate, unemotional,
free from needless noise. A word of counsel from
the old men answered most of the purposes for which,
in our modern communities, we maintain courts.

Of course, Laughs-at-the-Sky did not go to school,
for such an institution was unknown among his peo-

ple. Of what we call learning there was none. In
the absence of an alphabet and an articulated written language, there were only pictures and symbolic
designs, with either an historical record or a spiritual
reminder in view. So far from having to learn to
read and write and cipher in order to hold their own
against their neighbors in trade, the red folk were
accustomed to go directly to the prime sources of
supply for food and raiment and shelter. The boy,
therefore, was taught to hunt and fish and set traps
for game; the girl was taught to cook and keep the
camp comfortable. Here we find vocational instruction and domestic science reduced to their very lowest terms.

Nor was the religious training of children neglected.
The red man's religion, however, was in every sense
a religion of nature. In detail, there were differences
between the faiths of different tribes, but natural
phenomena furnished the foundations of all of them.
Magnitude, grandeur, power, were the attributes which
most strongly moved the imagination of the aborigine
and stirred in him the impulse of worship. To a great
wind, a flood, a huge boulder, a livid cloud, he would
pray in order that its terrors might be averted from
his camp. The sun was, to the majority of the Indians, the embodiment of Deity, because it played so
large a part in everything on which they depended
for support and enjoyment.

Back of all these images, it is true, there lurked
in the minds of the more advanced tribes a vague
notion of an invisible, intangible, inscrutable essence
—the Great Spirit, or the Great White Spirit, as we

find it described in literature. But the broader ethical phases of what we understand by religion appear to have been attached very loosely to, rather than interwoven with, these ancient faiths. One's duty to one's fellows was obviously a subject to be considered by itself, and the Indian's ethical philosophy grew largely out of his social environment. A peaceable disposition, soft words, a gentle voice and manner, liberality —all these were, in such a society as that in which he lived, necessary to the common comfort; so the wise Indian endured an occasional injustice with unruffled front, rather than risk all that the opposite course might bring upon him. By this I do not mean that Laughs-at-the-Sky grew up in ignorance of what a quarrel meant. Among the red men of old, as among other races then and since, there were many individuals who disregarded the ideals they had always been taught to revere. But the tone and temper given to an Indian camp generally by those ideals made it as harmonious and restful a dwelling-place as the world probably has ever seen.

In another and very practical direction, young Laughs-at-the-Sky received a good training. He had to know how to take care of himself in the daily struggle with the forces of nature and the occasional contest with human enemies which would fall to his lot in manhood; and this involved his early learning not only how to follow trails and shoot, propel a boat and fish, but also how to practice various simple handicrafts. He must be able to select the right pliant wood for his bow and the right rigid wood for his arrows, and to fashion these with implements

made of sharpened stone and bones. In giving the
bow just the best temper, he might have to cover it
with moist earth and build a fire on top of the mound
to bring about the desired steaming. The production
of fire was itself an art. Whether the use of flint
for this purpose was ever general among the red men
till the whites introduced them to it, I am far from
sure; but every aged Indian who has talked with me
about the customs of his childhood has described the
use of the fire-stick, a long piece of wood held ver-
tically between the palms and made to rotate with
great velocity, the sharp point of the lower end being
fitted into an indentation in another and larger piece
laid flat on the ground. Around the edge of the
indentation would be sprinkled powdered dry grass,
which would ignite as soon as the friction caused by
twirling the stick had evolved a spark.

Not only bows and arrows but bludgeons and spear-
handles had to be fashioned of wood of various sorts,
the maker's skill being put to proof both in the selec-
tion of the material and in its preliminary treatment
and final shaping. The arrows and spears had to
have heads of stone; and a favorite war weapon was
the tomahawk, a crude mixture of battle-ax and club,
with a heavy stone blade or knob. The bow must be
strung, and the heads of the other appliances securely
fastened to the shafts; and for these, as for all purposes of tying, or lashing, or sewing, the only twine
employed was made of the sinews of some large animal, like a deer. The seasoning of sinews, and their
winding and knotting while in the best state of plas-
ticity, required considerable study. In short, Laughs-

at-the-Sky had to be educated into an all-around artisan while still young and adaptable. His sister, meanwhile, was drilled in the common household duties, and taught how to tan skins and sew them together for clothing and tent-coverings, not omitting some attention to the decorative side of her work, as a preparation for becoming mistress of the camp of her future husband.

As the lad grew up, he was fortified for the more active undertakings of manhood by subjection to various ordeals. If there were a secret society in his tribe to which he desired admission, he had to pass through an initiatory ceremonial of which flogging, or some other painful bodily experience, was a prominent feature. Or possibly he might be sent into the wilderness to live for a long period, entirely isolated from his kind. Here he was supposed to commune with the spirits of earth and air, and to give his mind the necessary philosophic bent by silent meditation and self-scrutiny. He was obliged to fast, or to subsist on wild berries and barks, being permitted to carry with him neither food nor any weapon suitable for killing game. Indeed, in some tribes it was the custom, when a youth on the verge of maturity was sent off on this lonesome errand, to proclaim him virtually an outlaw for the time, so that any one who chose was at liberty to slay him and inherit whatever special privileges might be in store for him. A part of the purpose underlying this provision appears to have been educative in a very practical way, since the person undergoing the ordeal, appreciating the peril to which he was exposed, would draw upon all his mother-wit to study out plans for concealment and escape from a pursuing enemy; the resourcefulness thus acquired might one day stand him in excellent stead in actual warfare.

Other devices, showing great ingenuity in the contrivance of methods of torture, were conjured up with a view to putting the youth's courage, and the steadiness of his nerves, to a crucial test, before which he must succumb unless divinely marked for a career. These trials also cultivated in him, if he proved worthy, a stolidity of demeanor which would qualify him, when captured alive by a hostile force, to defy them to their faces, exchange taunt for taunt with them, and chant a death-song with unfaltering voice even while they were filling his body with arrows or lighting a funeral pyre under his feet.

Having satisfied the elders of his tribe that he deserved their confidence, Laughs-at-the-Sky was admitted to the councils in which measures of tribal government and policy were discussed. To our modern notion these gatherings appear very informal, but they were conducted according to certain unwritten laws as well recognized and respected as our familiar code of parliamentary procedure. The general rule, " Young men for action, old men for counsel," was uniformly observed, and lay at the basis of all the proceedings. The old men opened the talk, their juniors keeping quiet till the last of the patriarchs had had his say. As might be imagined, a people as close to nature as our red men in their primitive state made large use of natural phenomena in their figures of speech, and drew upon these continually for illustrations in support of their arguments. The practice gave that strong poetic and picturesque flavor to their oratory which so deeply impressed the minds of our early white explorers. The young men, it is almost needless to say, were more fiery than the old ones. They were, as a rule, ambitious to win chieftainship by waging war, or raiding a rival tribe, whenever a promising opportunity offered. The advice of the old men was usually in the direction of patience, and a careful consideration of possible consequences before taking heavy chances with a foe whose strength was unascertained.

Whatever may be our opinion of his manner of expressing it, no one can deny that the primitive Indian had a deeply religious nature. As he recognized the divine essence in everything about him, he embarked on no enterprise without invoking the approval and assistance of the Deity, and this custom was carried to extreme lengths now and then. To our minds, for instance, there is something fatally incongruous in the idea of asking a blessing upon an expedition, under cover of night, to steal a hostile neighbor's property. But, according to the code of the ancient Americans, an enemy was fair prey at all times; any damage which could not be done to him in open combat might be done just as well on the sly, since the rule of their competition was not only force for force, but trick for trick. For a hunting party there was always a devotional exercise by way of preparation; but the great occasion for such a demonstration was the outset of a band of warriors for the field of battle. Before eating and before sleeping, every man was instructed to pray for strength for himself and the common victory, and the leader must offer sacrifices for his whole command. Often a war party would continue all night in prayer, and burn incense of pine gum and sweet grass to purify themselves. Any one of the number who wished to render his petitions particularly acceptable might make a sacrifice of some of his own hair or flesh, or scourge and stab himself till the blood flowed copiously, or even apply red-hot coals to his skin without wincing, to prove his worthiness.

So, as Laughs-at-the-Sky bloomed into full manhood and began to take his share in the work of his tribe, he found himself in a religious atmosphere which could not fail to have its effect on him throughout his later life. Dancing was almost invariably an accompaniment of invocations of divine favor. The Indian dance was a wholly different thing from any performance of the same name among our people. There was nothing at all graceful about it, and pairing off the sexes was unknown. In many of the dances the women bore no part, unless it might be to join in the singing; to others they contributed some motion, perhaps standing in a circle and alternately rising on the balls of their feet and settling back again, as they turned slowly around and around in time with the music; this was vocal, punctuated with rhythmic beats on the tom-tom and shakes of the rattle.

Most of the dances were symbolic, and not infrequently the symbolism involved those mysteries of nature which our modern taste reserves for the privacy of very intimate intercourse. No such discriminations disturbed the mind of the aborigine. His fables gave animal attributes to the sun and the earth and the rain, and wove a conceit, half poetic and half literal, about the scattering of the seed, and the germination and development of the plant, and the gradual maturing of the fruit, which was interpreted in dramatic symbols in some of his dances in celebration of the spring sowing and the autumn harvest. It is on such typifications that most of the objections to Indian dances first arose. Other grounds for disapproving them I shall notice elsewhere.

In due course, Laughs-at-the-Sky followed the custom of his people, and sought a wife. How he went about his courtship depended on what tribe he belonged to, for every group of Indians had its own way of doing such things. In nearly all instances the preliminary arrangements were conducted by the parents of the young man. The proposal of marriage might be suggested by him, but his family sat in council over the matter. If they liked the girl he had chosen and thought the union between the two families desirable, they opened negotiations with the parents of the girl, and on her side in turn a domestic council took the question under consideration. All going well, the next thing was to announce the approaching wedding in the camp. There were no newspapers in which to advertise it, so it sometimes fell to the girl herself to do this by carrying every day to the tent in which the young man lived a portion of food of her own cooking, which she laid before him as she expected to continue laying food before him through their married lives together. Or, in those tribes in which the woman owned the dwelling, and the bridegroom attached himself to the bride's family instead of making the bride a part of his, this order would be reversed, the young man visiting the girl's home bearing tributes of one kind or another till the day arrived for the actual nuptials. Beyond a feast or some similar social gathering, there was rarely any specific celebration of the marriage, certainly no solemn ceremony like that to which we are accustomed. Wedding gifts were commonly abundant, the friends of both families trying to set the young couple up with all the practical necessaries of housekeeping.

In some tribes, marriage by purchase was the rule. The young man's family would present the young woman's family with handsome gifts in consideration of their consent to the match; and, although it was often denied in later years that this was the price paid for the bride, a pretty sure sign that it was appears in the fact that, in some of these tribes, even to our day, the return of part or all of the gifts is demanded in case the woman tires of her husband and leaves him. Divorce was about as simple a matter as marriage. Among certain groups of Indians the husband's will in such affairs was law, and the woman was cast off without further ado, and without the necessity of assigning a cause. Among others, the man was powerless, but the wife could divorce him and turn him out of their dwelling on any pretext she chose. Between these extreme cases came a few where either party who was dissatisfied would simply slip out of the house without warning, and the party thus deserted was thenceforth free to choose another mate.

No family can hope to escape illness altogether, and the household of Laughs-at-the-Sky and his wife was not free from it. For obvious reasons their troubles were not of the sort which flow from over-indulgence in rich foods, or from lack of fresh air and exercise, but grew out of imprudences and accidents hardly separable from such a life as they led in the wilds. No family physician and no telephone being available, a messenger was sent to the nearest medicine-man, who, under the inspiration of gifts of great value, proceeded to perform various incantations over the patient, sometimes accompanied by the songs and dances of a party of Indians called in for the purpose. Simple ailments this practitioner could handle very well. Although, for the sake of keeping up the illusion as to his magical powers, he would go through a deal of mummery which had no outward relation to the disorder he had been bidden to cure, he showed much skill in administering cathartics, soporifics, tonics, sweating medicines, expectorants, kidney excitants, emetics, and poultices for inflamed mucous surfaces. All his most valuable medicines he prepared from herbs and roots found in waste places, which had been proved by experiment through several generations to be capable of producing certain definite effects. He knew also how to extract barbed arrows from the flesh, reduce sprains, and dress open wounds, though he had no idea how to set a broken bone so as to insure his patient against permanent crippling.

MEDICINE CHIEFS PREPARING FOR THE DANCE.

If the malady were internal but refused to yield to the crude medicaments at his command, the medicine-man would probably tell the patient that his sufferings were caused by an invisible bear or other fierce brute which was gnawing at his vitals. This evil spirit could be frightened away only by a noisy and pretty expensive ceremony of exorcism. The din of the ordeal would have driven a normal person of our race half frantic, but the patient and his family were willing to endure anything for the sake of the promised benefit. When a victim survived it and recovered, the sorcerer attributed the happy outcome to his own necromantic arts; if not, he declared the failure due to his having been called in too late, after a mortal injury had been inflicted by the controlling demon.

On one of the forays of his tribe, Laughs-at-the-Sky perhaps performed some exploit of uncommon valor, like wrenching from the grasp of an antagonist, in a hand-to-hand struggle on the battle-field, a huge bow made of elk's horn, so heavy and so stiff that none but its owner, a man of giant strength, had ever before been able to use it. Laughs-at-the Sky astonished his comrades as well as the enemy by bending it and sending a deadly arrow through the body of the warrior from whom he had wrested it, and who had started to flee immediately upon the loss of the weapon. Thenceforward our hero was known among his fellows no longer by the name given him at his birth, but as " the young man who captured the big bow "—or, by a literal translation of the Indian contraction for this phrase, as Young-Big-Bow.

It is not essential to our present purpose to follow
him through all the adventures and experiences of his
later life, which merely rang the changes on hunting and warfare, warfare and hunting. The next distinctive event in his history was its finale. He had
grown old slowly, but had not failed to realize the
passing of his powers, and at last found himself face
to face with death. There was nothing terrifying to
him in the discovery. Many of his old friends had
gone this way before, and he was ready for his summons to fall into the procession. As he felt the end
approaching he gathered his family about him for a
leave-taking. There was no lawyer to draw his will;
but by word of mouth he disposed of his most cherished treasures—the bow and arrows he had stripped
from the chieftain slain by his own hand, his shield
of buffalo hide, the decorated spear he had inherited
from his father, his war-bonnet gorgeous with stained
eagle-feathers, the tools of wood and stone he had
employed in his simple handicrafts. Then those who
were nearest and dearest to him fulfilled their parting offices. They oiled and combed and braided his
hair, painted his face with a red pigment, brought new
clothing in which to wrap his form, and provided generally for his meeting the coming visitant with proper
dignity.

As he closed his eyes upon the scenes of earth,
he had the vision-laden hour which comes to all man-
kind while the body is loosing its hold on the spirit.
But the pictures which rose before his mind were not
of a splendid city with streets of gold and gates of
pearl, or of a river on whose opposite bank the father

and mother, the wife and children who had already crossed were waiting to welcome him. What he saw was a peaceful plain of green prairie-grass, where the game was always plentiful and fat, and the tents of a happy people dotted the foreground with pyramids of white and gray. This favored spot may have been somewhere above the clouds, but surely in the direction of the setting sun, and possibly beyond the great seas which bounded his western horizon with a barrier of mystery. Many and many a time, as he was returning to his camp after a day's absence, he had watched the sun sinking to rest and the soft mists rising between him and it, and wondered what lay beyond. It was a wonder mixed never with fear but always with confidence. Such a thing as atheism was unknown among the red men. They were content not to define the character and qualities of the Great Spirit who absorbed and animated all the lesser spirits in nature, but to rest calm in the assurance that whatever the future held in store for them had been ordered for their well-being.

It may be that hours, or days, or even weeks elapsed between the preparations for death and its actual coming. When, however, the old man had heaved his last sigh, the assembled mourners began their wailing. His closest friends cut their hair short at the neck, and gashed their bodies with knives in token of their grief. Some went so far as to cut off two or three fingers at the first joint, so that the maimed hand might keep them always in memory of their loss. One group of mourners stayed near the body, chanting and groaning; another sought an elevated point

near by, and voiced their sorrow to the sky. When
these functions had been carried to a length befitting
the prominence of the departed, the formal funeral
began.

In a wrapping made of home-tanned skin or of
the pliable bark of a tree, the corpse was carried to
its place of sepulture. If the weather would permit,
a rude grave was dug in the earth and it was laid
away therein with a pipe and tobacco, some fire-mak-
ing implements, a bow and arrows for hunting, and
enough food to subsist a traveler on a journey of
several days. If the earth were frozen too hard to
dig, the body was stretched on the surface and a
low hut of saplings and bark was built over it; or
perhaps it was perched in the air on a scaffold of
poles. The medicine-men took charge of the final
rites and, on the march from the tepee to the burial-
place, their leader chanted a song designed to drive
away devils, beating on his tom-tom as an accompaniment and to measure the tread of the line of mourners.
The speech of the occasion was made by the most
notable orator in the band. He addressed the silent
figure of his late associate, recounting his deeds of
prowess, enumerating the scalps he had brought back
from the wars, extolling his many acts of kindness
to his fellow-tribesmen, and recalling his words of
wise and timely counsel.

Then the head medicine-man bade the dead Indian
a last farewell, prophesying his success in finding the
trail to the happy hunting-ground, but warning him
that it was narrow and obscure, and so beset by evil
spirits that he must keep his eyes always fixed on

it, looking neither backward nor to the right or left, lest he be tempted into a pitfall. To this admonition the other medicine-men responded in a chorus which was supposed to convey the dead man's assurance that he was proceeding peacefully on his long journey toward the setting sun, and looking forward to the joys which awaited him when he should have finished it. A general acclaim of satisfaction from the listening throng brought the ceremony to a close.

Here we, too, take leave of our friend, the red man as he was of old, before the invading heralds of an alien civilization had undertaken to transform him into something better—or worse. It is fortunate for his descendants that in our bustling era a few students are patiently gathering such facts about him as are still obtainable after the lapse of so many generations; for it is necessary to know as much as we can of the Indian of yesterday, in order to understand the Indian of to-day and to protect the Indian of to-morrow.

II

THE RED MAN AND THE GOVERNMENT

He that ruleth over men must be just.—2 Samuel 23:3.

Brothers, we have seen how great a people the whites are. They are very rich and very strong. It is folly for us to fight them. We shall go home with much knowledge. For myself, I shall advise my people to be quiet and live like good men. The advice which you gave us, brother, is very good, and we tell you now we intend to walk the straight path in future, and to content ourselves with what we have, and with cultivating our lands.—BLACK HAWK, *the Sauk Leader*.

II

THE RED MAN AND THE GOVERNMENT

ALTHOUGH the red men within the United States proper—that is, in the area bounded by Canada and Mexico and the two great oceans—number about one in every three hundred of the total population, the federal government has not, till within very recent years, had an Indian policy worthy the name. After the war of the Revolution, the tendency of the white people to move from the eastern coast westward suggested the importance of establishing definite relations with those tribes that might oppose their progress, but nobody appears to have mapped out a comprehensive plan of procedure. In a broad way, the idea was to hold peace parleys with all alike; then, those who showed a hospitable spirit were to be kept in good humor by gifts, and instructed in agriculture and kindred arts; those who were unfriendly, but not powerful enough to drive back the white immigrants, were to be subdued by warfare and civilized in captivity; and those with whom it seemed impracticable to do anything else were to be destroyed, root and branch. The first step in this crude program called for the negotiation of " treaties."

Following a practice begun by the several colonies in earliest times, the tribes were dealt with as so

many independent "nations," whose "kings" were
qualified to make and receive pledges for them;
and the treaties bear evidence, in their grandiose
phraseology, of the solemnity which the government
of the new republic wished to attach to their contents. Most of these instruments concerned cessions of lands which the government had recognized, formally at least, the right of the Indians to
occupy. Of course, in a country unsurveyed and
largely unknown to the invading race, the descrip-
tions of the ceded tracts needs must be inexact and
unsatisfactory. The difference between the English
tongue, with its copious vocabulary and its abundant
provisions for expressing delicate shades of meaning,
and the rough, elemental languages of the Indians,
who had no written forms and whose main use for
words was to make a few simple wants known to
each other, further complicated the work of treaty-
making; so that the product, if later events required
its more careful analysis, was found often to convey one meaning to the Indian negotiators and quite
another to the whites. When we add to these difficulties the fact that not seldom the honesty of the
interpreters employed was open to question, we can
see why many of the cases in which the government
has been charged with deliberate duplicity are capable
of explanation as the result of misunderstandings.

Another feature of these transactions, which were
always perilous and occasionally tragic, was the ignorance of the Indians regarding the lawful methods of
our government. A treaty with them was entered
into, on behalf of the United States, by the President,

but, as in the case of treaties with foreign powers, required ratification by the Senate, and sometimes the passage of an act of Congress, before it could become effective. In one notable instance, in California, a large number of Indians signed away their homes on the understanding that the government was to provide them with others, but the Senate postponed action on the treaties; the Indians, assuming that the preliminaries were complete, proceeded to move out; a land-hungry mob of whites at once moved in and took possession; and the Indians became wanderers, homeless and hopeless, because the executive branch of the government had not the courage to interfere and drive the white squatters away till the Senate could find time to act and other habitations for the red men could be hunted up. As it was, the Senate never did act; the treaties were discovered among a lot of other dust-covered rubbish in its pigeon-holes many years afterward, and a part of my administration was spent in buying such homes as we could for the unfortunates who had been without any for a whole generation.

The practice of treaty-making finally became so sorry a farce that Congress abolished it by law; and since 1871 "agreements" have taken the place of treaties in dealings between the government and the Indians. It is hard for any one with a conscience which takes more note of principles than of phrases, to see what distinction can fairly be drawn here; but what actually happened was that Congress began to take all sorts of liberties with such negotiations from that day forward. The agreements were always framed at councils between certain white negotiators and the leaders of a tribe, and then sent to Congress for its action. If Congress was not satisfied with the form in which an agreement was drawn, instead of sending it back to the parties who drew it and advising that such-and-such changes be made in the text, it would simply make the changes itself without consulting anybody, and pass a bill " to ratify an agreement with" the tribe, as if the contents of the bill were the same as the contents of the agreement. Naturally, this was not to the taste of the Indians concerned; and when it had gone on for some thirty years in disregard of repeated protests, an especially flagrant case brought about a momentous lawsuit. An act was passed, ostensibly to ratify an agreement with the Kiowa, Comanche, and Apache Indians, opening to settlement a large part of their lands, and, as this legislation embodied sundry features absolutely at variance with the agreement it purported to confirm, the Indian Rights Association raised a test case by trying to sue out an injunction. The fight was carried all the way up to the Supreme Court, which decided, on January 5, 1903, that " the power exists [in Congress] to abrogate the provisions of an Indian treaty," and that " its action is conclusive" beyond the power of the judicial arm of the government to intervene. Since that day no time and energy have been squandered on making agreements with Indians for cessions of land or anything else, but Congress legislates regarding their so-called property as freely as if it belonged unreservedly to the government.

Owing to the hostile clashes which were continually occurring between the white communities and the red men on the frontier, the handling of Indian affairs at large was at the outset entrusted to the War Department. From the foundation of the government till 1824 the Secretary of War dealt with the Indians directly; but in that year he organized a Bureau of Indian Affairs within his department. With various minor changes, this arrangement continued till 1849, when the Department of the Interior was created and the Indian Bureau was transferred to it, with a Commissioner at its head whose appointment was vested in the President and subject to confirmation by the Senate. Up to that time the chief work of the Bureau had consisted of regulating trade between whites and Indians, making such distributions of goods and money to the several tribes as the government had promised them, and trying to maintain friendly relations, with an occasional draft upon the army for assistance. This will account for many of the incongruous provisions in old laws affecting Indian relations, which, though dead letters for all practical purposes, remain still unrepealed. To a person who should read the existing statutes at length without knowing the history behind them, they would be almost unintelligible. They need a thorough overhauling by a commission of experts, and reduction to a compact and comprehensive code. As they stand now, there is not a duty they require the government to perform which can safely be undertaken without first running back through the records to ascertain whether it is assignable to the President, to the Secretary of the Interior, to the Secretary of War, to the Commissioner of Indian Affairs, to two of these officers jointly, or to one with the approval or at the instance of another.

Sometimes a subject is so muddled as to suggest possibilities of a sensational conflict of authority. For example: the Secretary of the Interior, one of whose duties is to distribute funds due to Indian tribes, is forbidden to make such a distribution when there is reason "to believe there is any species of intoxicating liquors within convenient reach of the Indians"; but it is the War Department, and not the Department of the Interior, that is empowered to grant permits for carrying liquor into the Indian country; while the duty of removing from a reservation any person whose presence there seems "detrimental to the peace and welfare of the Indians" devolves upon the Commissioner.

Now, imagine what might happen if the Secretary of the Interior wished to make a payment to the Indians on a certain reservation, but learned that there were intoxicating liquors on the ground, in the possession of somebody who held a permit from the Secretary of War. The payment might be overdue, and the Indians might be restless and liable to make trouble unless they received their money promptly; yet the Secretary of the Interior would have no actual right to drive off the owners of the liquor as persons whose presence was detrimental to the peace and welfare of the tribe, that function being not his but the Commissioner's. If the Commissioner were unwilling to act, the Secretary would have no right to issue

NAVAJO HOME (A Rug in Process).

a peremptory command to him regarding a matter which the statute places primarily in his discretion; if the Secretary should issue such a command and the Commissioner should refuse to obey it, the Secretary is not empowered to dismiss or otherwise punish him for contumacy, because he is the President's and not the Secretary's appointee. If, on the other hand, the Commissioner sympathized with the Secretary's desire to rid the reservation of the presence of persons with liquor in their possession, and set in motion the proceedings for doing this, we should be treated to the spectacle of a subordinate officer issuing an order, with the approval of one member of the President's Cabinet, overriding the order of another Cabinet member issued under the sanction of an act of Congress. Of course, this is only a hypothetical case, unlikely ever to happen; but it would nevertheless be entirely possible under the absurd patchwork of law which has been continued in force long after the conditions that called its inconsistencies into being have passed away. I have chosen it from among a multitude of illustrations which might be cited, because it will explain in some degree the demand for a thorough revision of existing statutes. Not till this modernizing process is complete shall we be able, when anything goes wrong, to place the blame promptly at the door where it belongs.

Although the Commissioner is next in official rank to the Secretary of the Interior, the latter has his staff of Inspectors whose duty it is to keep him informed of what is going on in and under the Indian

Bureau, including the conduct of the Commissioner himself. Under the Commissioner, in turn, is a staff of secondary inspecting officers, known variously as Supervisors and Special Agents, through whom he derives his information of how things are moving in the outside field. Substantially the whole Indian population, as we shall see later, is settled on reservations. Over every reservation presides a functionary who in old times was known as an Indian Agent, and who was appointed by the President with the concurrence of the Senate. By degrees the civil service rules have been applied to Indian agencies, and the functions assigned to Agents are now performed by Superintendents of local Indian schools, whose appointments, promotions, and transfers are made, or are supposed to be made, on grounds of merit alone. The purpose of this change was to remove the Indian service from the domination of partisan politics, with the incidental abuses thereof. While such evils may not have been eliminated under the new régime, they have undoubtedly been reduced to a minimum, partly by narrowing the openings for wrongdoing, partly by procuring a higher average class of men for the positions, and partly by bringing the whole force more closely under the control of the Secretary, who makes the appointments and administers penalties for malfeasance. Also, it has had a salutary influence on the Indians by associating in their minds the educational system with the sources of general authority.

It is in order now to go back and see how the Indians became possessed of specific reservations, instead of roaming at large over all the western wilderness as of old. Indian reservations are areas set apart by the government for the sole occupancy of a tribe or tribes, or of one or more fragments of tribes, the land in every reservation being, at the outset, held in common by the tribal members. This system was established originally as an expedient for pushing Indian disturbers out of the path of white immigration and permitting the peaceful development of new country by the incomers. The belief was general, in the earlier half of the last century, that the only way to avoid collisions between the white and the red races was to keep them as far apart as possible; and some of our statesmen of that period entertained the hope that the more progressive Indians had already absorbed enough of the spirit which animated the white citizens to wish to imitate them in self-government. So an experiment on a large scale was undertaken by carving out of the public domain an " Indian Territory " some distance west of the Mississippi River, transporting thither five tribes which had been occupying lands in five of the southeastern states, and setting them up in business as a sort of red men's republic. The place chosen was, at that time, so far beyond where anybody dreamed that our civilization would ever extend, that it was assumed the Indians would always be free from interference by other races.

The attempt proved a dismal failure. The Indians showed no natural inclination to self-rule, at least in the form prescribed for them; the government's proclamation that they were to be independent was an invitation to every white outlaw in the Southwest, fleeing from justice in any of the states, to take refuge in Indian Territory as the one place where he could be secure from arrest; and by degrees the condition of things there became so unbearably corrupt and dangerous that the government was forced to make a complete reorganization. This was done under the forms of agreements negotiated with the five tribes; but actually it was a plain taking-over of the territory, its reduction to the status of other territories, and finally its erection into a state, under the name Oklahoma.

The other tribes had in the meantime been distributed through the great West on reservations, where no attempt was made to teach them self-government, but where they could more easily be kept out of trouble among themselves, protected against the evil designs of outsiders if their Agents were active and honest, and instructed in farming by teachers appointed by the Bureau in Washington. This plan, however, proved as mistaken on the side of excessive paternalism as the Indian Territory experiment had on the side of excessive liberty. Congress fell into the habit of legislating about details which might better have been left to the judgment of the administrative officers in charge, though persistently refusing or neglecting to provide by law the means of handling certain crises of real importance which were liable to occur without warning. As a bribe to the Indians to remain quiet, rations of food and clothing, or sums of money were distributed among them at certain intervals. Between the necessity for buying all the material supplies by contract, and the fact

that, when money was given, the Indians were ignorant of how much should come to them, or how to
count it after payment, or how to receipt for it except
with a cross-mark of whose significance they had only
the most hazy notion, this system presently became
a prolific breeder of scandals, in which figured the
bad quality of goods furnished, false weights and
measures, favoritism in the distributions, and the jug-
gling of accounts. For many years the agencies were
so far from civilization that inspection was impracticable, except at rare intervals, and investigations
were almost prohibitively expensive. And not only
did the Indians become pauperized through their gra-
tuities, but they learned the trick of stirring the government to greater liberality now and then by threats
of a bloody outbreak.

In size, reservations varied from a few hundred acres
to several million. Of those which are left still un-
broken, the Navajo reservation in Arizona, New
Mexico, and Utah is the largest, embracing nearly
fifteen thousand square miles. They differ quite as
widely in fertility of soil and mineral wealth, the
Osage reservation being thus far the richest for agriculture, stock-raising, and oil production. When a
body of Indians were settled on a reservation they
were forbidden to leave it, except on written passes
issued by their Agent, and all outsiders were forbidden to enter it unless they had first made their business known and received express permission. Trade
within a reservation was restricted with equal care.
Any resident Indian might buy, or sell, or barter to
his heart's content, but white merchants were allowed

to set up stores only by special license. The privilege was a monopoly granted to but few in any event; and those few must produce, as a prerequisite, proofs of good character and financial responsibility, and give bond to obey the laws and regulations. In recent years the West has been so much more closely settled that these rules have been relaxed, and Indians are generally encouraged to do their trading in nearby towns which offer any advantages over the licensed stores; so the reservation privilege has fallen in favor and is little sought.

As the President could not possibly know personally all the Agents he had to appoint, he fell back upon the Senators and Representatives for recommendations of fit men, and thus grew up a vicious practice of patronage. By this I do not mean that all, or even a majority, of the appointees were morally bad men; but citizens who could be sure of a good living by their independent efforts at home were, as a rule, loath to go away from everything they prized and bury themselves in the wilds for a brief term of years at salaries contemptibly small. Hence, it is not wonderful that so many candidates for agencies were minor politicians whose chief claim to notice was some service rendered in a recent campaign, but who were not capable of administering any office requiring high business qualifications, or who had worn out their influence at home so that they could no longer be of much usefulness to their party there. In command of their reservations, such men usually gave their chief thought to getting through their prescribed course of duty with as little effort or worry as possible.   Included with their other unsuitable traits might be an element of cowardice; and, in order to put on a mask of bravado which they believed would awe the Indians into harmlessness, they were sometimes very cruel.   They could be so with comparatively little fear of exposure, for in early days the Indians could not communicate with Washington except through their Agents, and then only as tribes and not as individuals; and if a complaint ever got past an Agent, his word in denial carried a great deal more weight than theirs.   Whatever may or may not have been the prevalence of abuses, the system was distinctly unwholesome; and the growing disgust of the public with such of its unpleasant fruits as cropped above the surface led to the changes already described.

Meanwhile, a process of evolution had been going on in land matters.   The abnormalities of the reservation policy so impressed the late Henry L. Dawes, then a Senator from Massachusetts and a generous student of the Indian question, that he procured the passage of the general allotment act of 1887.   The plan which he proposed to inaugurate on a broad scale had already been tried on a narrow one by special laws affecting a few single tribes.   The Dawes law empowered the President, whenever in his judgment any tribe had reached a stage of development which would warrant such a change, to carve up its reservation, and allot to every man, woman, and child thereon a separate and individual farm of forty, eighty, or one hundred and sixty acres—the area being decided according to sundry variable conditions needless to enumerate here—and to issue to the allottee a patent for this farm, by the terms of which the government was to hold it in trust for him for twenty-five years and then present him with a title in fee. In the interval, by virtue of his receiving the trust patent, he became invested with all the privileges of a citizen, except the right to sell or encumber his land, which the trust also exempted from taxation. The theory was that the Indian would thus be assured of a home and the means of self-support; that he would come to be regarded, and to regard himself, as a distinct person, instead of a mere infinitesimal and undivided part of a tribal whole; that his vote would command attention to his wants from politicians who had long been accustomed to ride over him unscrupulously; and that the twenty-five years' life of the trust would be utilized practically as a period of education and probation, during which he would fit himself for the responsibilities of land-ownership and independence.

Some of these expectations were realized, but with incidentals which no one could have foreseen. It was true that Indians who could vote soon enjoyed a degree of attention from the politicians quite unknown to Indians who could not vote; but this meant also that they furnished fresh victims for the corruptionist, who was not long in learning how to buy and sell their votes, at wholesale or retail, as freely as the votes of a corresponding class of ignorant citizens of any other race. Farming had become, on the dry plains of the West, so elaborate an art as to tax the ingenuity even of white men of pretty well-trained intelligence, and descended from ancestors who had always had problems to master in competition with others in their own lines of fortune-seeking; so it was not wonderful that, with nothing in their own experience to prepare them and no inherited equipment for tackling such difficulties, and with markets for their surplus products too remote to be of any real avail, many of the Indians found agriculture a precarious means of livelihood and gradually gave it up in discouragement.*

The land left after all the Indians on a reservation had been allotted was usually sold to settlers, who, bringing with them their own ways of working and living, not only developed the neighborhood but set an example to those Indians who still desired to become farmers.   Other whites, who did not care to buy, rented farms from allottees for an annual stipend. The government consented to this in the cases of unmarried women, widows, children, defectives, and any who were too old to work, but frowned upon leasing by able-bodied men, many of whom nevertheless contrived to outwit their custodians, lease their lands, and live in idleness on the rents.

* Conditions are reported to have been somewhat relieved of late by a system of reimbursable appropriations, which began five or six years ago with an experiment at the Fort Belknap Agency in Montana, and has since spread to a few other reservations.   It contemplates the appropriation by Congress of a certain sum to be spent on implements, seed, and other farming necessaries which the Indians concerned have not the capital to procure; these are distributed on the understanding that they are to be paid for from the proceeds of the farms on which they are used.   The plan has not been in operation long enough to justify a sweeping verdict on its efficacy, but hopeful reports come from some of the Superintendents who have had the disbursing of funds to their own Indians.

Lack of employment meant, for these men, falling into bad ways. Gambling, always a favorite vice among primitive peoples, afforded excitement in an atmosphere generally lifeless and uninteresting; and there were always near a reservation plenty of rascals who stood ready to smuggle whiskey into the camps. Intoxication became a curse far more to be dreaded than gambling, for the Indian gamesters had little wealth to throw away; but their fiery drink drove them to deeds of violence and left a trail of disease and decadence wherever it was carried. Federal statutes, as well as local laws in most of the Western states, imposed serious penalties upon selling or giving liquor to Indians, and, as long as the red men remained absolutely dependent on the government, convictions could be got wherever the proofs were clear and judges and juries unbiased: but the citizenship conferred upon an allottee with his trust patent put quite another face on this matter. The point was promptly raised that the sale of liquor to a citizen within a state could not be punished by federal law. One dramseller who had been arrested and brought to trial under a federal statute for selling liquor to an Indian allottee carried his case, by appeal after appeal, to the United States Supreme Court, which settled the question forever by deciding in his favor.

The gross debauching of the Indian ballot, coupled with this defeat of all efforts of the government to protect an allottee from the liquor-dealers, attracted wide notice, and caused the enactment of an amendment to the Dawes allotment law, designated the Burke act in honor of the Representative from South

Dakota who engineered it through Congress.   The
new act postponed the citizenship of the Indian till
the government trust could be removed from his land
and he should receive his title in fee.   It also empowered the Secretary of the Interior, whenever satisfied
of the competence of an allottee to manage his own
affairs, to suspend the trust and give him his final
patent, thus clothing him with citizenship without
waiting for the expiration of the twenty-five years'
probation period.   Under this provision the government has been working since 1906.   The Indians enfranchised before the passage of the Burke amendment are, of course, unaffected by it; but, as far as
the authorities at Washington have been able to control conditions, all who have been enfranchised since
are persons of enough intelligence to have only themselves to blame if they lose their property or become
besotted.

To give the red man an equal chance with the
white in his struggle for existence, the government
added to its other benefactions an educational establishment.   On the theory that the way to train an
Indian was to take him during his childhood away
from the surroundings amid which he had been born,
bring him up as a white child is brought up, and trust
to his settling in one of the older communities to
follow a civilized calling, a number of large boarding-
schools have been planted at points more or less dis-
tant from the reservations, and parents have been induced to let their children be kept there for a term
of years.   Another plan has been to gather the children of a reservation into a boarding-school situated

within it, where they can be taught the habits of whites without being too far separated from their families to permit of an occasional reunion. Besides these institutions day-schools are maintained on many reservations, presided over by a single teacher with the assistance of a wife, husband, or companion. From these day-schools, it was at the outset the government's intention to graduate the pupils into the reservation boarding-schools, and thence into the non-reservation boarding-schools, the ranks of the promoted thinning gradually on the way up. As a matter of fact, this is not the way the system has worked out. The ambition of the large schools to keep their rolls full has too often led them into taking children indiscriminately, without reference to the smaller schools, so that there has been no really consistent order of progression. The school question is treated more at length in another chapter.

The Indians are commonly called the "wards of the Nation." This phrase had its origin in a judicial decision many years ago, in which an attempt was made to define the duty of the United States Government toward the native race. Although the theory of wardship may be made, by a very liberal interpretation of terms, to answer for general purposes, it does not meet all the needs of the situation. When an ordinary guardian takes forcible possession of the property of his wards at a price, and under conditions of payment fixed by himself, we scrutinize his conduct as open to the suspicion of fraud, and he has to make out an extremely good case in order to clear himself of this. He is obliged, also, to make a

MOQUI GIRLS (With Headdress Indicating Mariageable Age).

report from time to time to the court which gave
him his authority, and in a dozen other ways he is
made to feel that he is not in all respects his own
master.

None of these restrictions finds a parallel in the
position of the government when handling Indian
affairs. There is no one to question the sovereignty
of the government. Moreover, it is a composite
organism, destitute of a personality, so that responsibility for its acts is diffused and uncertain. The President can do nothing without the direction or permission of Congress. Both Congress and the President
are helpless before an adverse mandate of the courts.
But as the courts are themselves the creatures of Congress, with a scope of action distinctly prescribed by
statute, and as the judges who compose them are appointed by the President with the consent of the
Senate, there is absolutely no point at which we can
focus accountability upon any one of the three coör-
dinate branches. They are all parts of the same huge
machine, which works as a whole. Hence, if Congress decides that a certain tract of land occupied
by an Indian tribe is needed to accommodate the
influx of white immigration into that part of the
country, it has only to enact a law directing the proper
executive officers to take possession of it and dispose
of it to the newcomers on such and such terms.

Actually, its uniform course is to fix a certain
price which shall be paid the Indians for surrendering
the land: this is a concession to decency. But as its
power to fix a price is bounded by no maximum and
minimum, there is nothing which could prevent its

simple seizure of anything it chose, without compensation beyond furnishing some other place of abode for the dispossessed occupants. Even where a distinct contract has been entered into, by order of Congress, between the government and a body of Indians, for the payment of so much money in consideration of the relinquishment of so much land, there is no way of compelling the government to live up to its agreement against its will. A tribe cannot carry such a case into court unless Congress gives it permission to do so; and, when permission has been granted and the tribe has carried its claim all the way from the lowest to the highest court and received a final award for the full amount it demanded, Congress has still to appropriate the money to satisfy the judgment. No sheriff can seize the Capitol or the White House and sell it under the hammer, or force the gates of the Treasury vaults and help himself to enough of the money stored there to pay the creditors their due.

In short, no power on earth can compel the settlement of a debt, or the performance of a pledge, from the government to the Indians, except a sensitive public conscience. Does not this make the pretence of the relation of guardian and ward a trifle absurd? A moral obligation exists, it is true: the same that always exists between the strong and the weak. It is the obligation which makes cities establish hospitals, and states support asylums, and charity boards provide food and clothes and shelter for orphan children. It is the same force which has built up the free school system and keeps it going at the expense of the whole body of taxpayers, and it is inspired by precisely the same motive—an enlightened instinct of self-protection. In the case of the hospitals and asylums and schools, however, the beneficiaries are directly under the eyes of the benefactors; and to take care of the unfortunate, the unsound, and the ignorant is recognized as the only way the rest of the community can avert the evils which would flow from the increase of such classes in the midst of them. With the Indians it was different during the period when the existing relation grew up, the bulk of the white citizens being far separated from the bulk of the red dependents. As long as that separation continued, little or no heed was paid to the moral improvement of the Indians, or to their possible destiny. The uppermost thought in the minds of our government and people was to avoid bloodshed between the races, or, if it occurred, to turn it to profitable account by forcing the natives farther westward and taking away more of their land in reprisal.

Here, in a nutshell, is the story of the white man's advance and the red man's retreat. That story epitomizes the philosophy underlying the government's adoption of the airs of a guardian over the Indians. As their guardian, it disciplined them when they disregarded its admonitions; as their guardian, it took possession of large slices of their estate wherever it could claim that they were using their land unwisely and therefore would be better without it; as their guardian, it concluded that they were likely to grow faster in grace if their wild-game supply were cut off, and on this pretext compelled them to give up hunting and submit to be fed and clothed like paupers at public expense. None of its designs, however veiled with benevolence, was carried out without vigorous resistance on the part of the wards, and the expenditure of many lives and much money; and, as if to salve its conscience for all these sacrifices, the guardian government established a system of schools where coming generations of its wards could be taught to cope with the master race which had overcome their fathers.

Let us be entirely charitable, and throw no disparagement upon any good thing the government has essayed to do. Considering how it is handicapped at every turn by its own cumbrousness, perhaps the wonder is that it has done as well as it has. But, in all seriousness, it has proved the mistake of attempting to perform a purely human and sympathetic task by machinery—even the machinery of a great and good nation. As well might we deliver a family of children into the keeping of a mechanical mother or an automatic nurse!

III

THE RED MAN AND HIS WHITE NEIGHBOR

Better is a neighbor that is near than a brother far off.—Proverbs 27:10.

You know our practice: If a white man, in traveling through our country, enters one of our cabins, we warm him if he is cold, we give him meat and drink that he may allay his hunger and thirst, and spread soft furs for him to rest and sleep on. We demand nothing in return.

But if I go into a white man's house and ask for victuals and drink, they say, "Where is your money?" And if I have none they say, "Get out, you Indian dog!" You see, they have not yet learned the little good things our mothers taught us when we were children.—CHIEF CANESTOGO, *of the Onondagas.*

III

THE RED MAN AND HIS WHITE
NEIGHBOR

IN view of the traditional objection of the red
aborigines of this country to the invasion of
white men and to white manners and methods, it
is of interest to note how universally white is regarded among the Indians as the color of majesty,
supremacy, deity. The President of the United States
is the " Great White Father," and the Commissioner
of Indian Affairs the " Little White Father." The
sun-worshippers in the Southwest, who are always on
the watch for the second coming of Montezuma,
speak of him as their " Great White Brother Who
Lives in the East." Elsewhere one hears often a reference to a " Great White Spirit." The clouds which
conceal a benevolent deity are white; the Messiah, over
whose promised advent the northern plains Indians
went mad about twenty years ago, was white; and Indians who have been converted to Christianity have
told me that they were now " praying to the White
God," as distinguished from the god or gods they
formerly worshipped.

The superior powers they recognize in the white
people seem to most Indians neither the cause nor
the effect of the whiteness, but merely its concomitant:

the Great Spirit, they say, looked with special favor upon one branch of the human race, and endowed it simultaneously with a white skin and with the art of "making big medicine"—that is, of doing wonderful things. Here we have, reduced to its simplest terms, the Indian mode of accounting for gunpowder and repeating rifles, steam machinery, electrical devices, great structures of masonry and metals, and, in general, the harnessing of nature's forces to obey the will of men; it is all "big medicine"—something to inspire awe, but not to provoke a hopeless attempt at emulation. Hence, the Indian, instead of trying, like the negro, to copy his white neighbors, has usually stood aloof, maintaining a position in which a dignified recognition of the superior inventive genius of the white race is mixed with an assertion of his own equality in every other respect, and his entire content to remain as his Creator made him.

Although in an earlier chapter, while trying to sketch in outline a picture of Indian life as it was before the whites poured into this country, I presented the tepee as the characteristic dwelling, it was only because this was the most common kind. There were several others. The Mandans of the Missouri Valley fixed heavy posts in position, laid cross timbers on these, and covered the whole with sod. The Comanches made their houses, as far as the framework was concerned, after the fashion of the tepee, but used as covering a heavy thatch of weeds and grass, so that one of their villages looked at a distance like a hayfield dotted with stacks. The Ojibways made theirs of poles and bark, in oblong shape,

INDIAN HOMES (Best of the New Type).

OJIBWAY TEPEES (Typical of the Passing Old Life).

with upright ends and a door in each end. The Iroquois followed generally the same style, but ran a long passage lengthwise of the hut with compartments opening out of it and places for fire at intervals. The Pueblo Indians used stone for their sidewalls, and boughs and saplings, plastered with a cement-like mud, for their roofs, and built their houses one against or above another in great clusters, thus effecting some of the same sort of economies in construction that we do when we build city dwellings in solid blocks, or apartment-houses grouping many suites together.

In every instance, it will be observed, material and design were dictated by environment and occupation. Where, for example, large game was most abundant, skins were employed for covering; and for convenience in hanging these, a conical structure of poles seemed fittest. Where there were forests, timber and bark entered more into the making of a dwelling. Where the prairie grass grew rank, the thatch came naturally into use; while on the broad stretches of desert clay, broken occasionally by buttes of stratified rock, the stone house was almost a necessity. Again, it should be noted that the tepee, the form of dwelling most readily movable, was used chiefly by the Indians who subsisted on several varieties of game, which had each to be sought on a different feeding-ground and at a different season of the year; for the house which could be picked up when the season changed, or when a new hunting region had to be visited, and shifted to a more convenient place, came nearest to an ideal abode. Whereas, among tribes whose pastoral or agricultural pursuits kept them almost all the time in one neighborhood, a more permanent dwelling was considered desirable.

For clothing, woven fabrics appear to have been not wholly unknown among some of the more advanced tribes, though the workmanship was crude in the extreme and much of the material was of sorts which have long since passed out of use, such as thin strips of hide, or strings made of twisted turkey feathers. The primitive Indian ate both animal and vegetable foods, but the animals were only such wild game as he could kill with the clumsy implements at his command, and the vegetable substances were the native products of forest and plain, like roots, berries, nuts, fungi, and seeds of various kinds. If any sporadic attempt was made to domesticate and breed animals for food purposes it seems to have been confined mainly to turkeys and dogs; and when, among tribes whose habits were sufficiently fixed to permit of it, the women took a little trouble to raise corn, beans, potatoes, and melons, their knowledge of how to care for them was only what their mothers had picked up from experiments and accident. Whenever it was practicable, food-stuffs were cooked in preference to eating them raw; but the cooking was elementary, often amounting to no more than parching or steaming. Where fuel was scarce, resort was had sometimes to hanging meats in the sun till they had either dried hard or become tender by semi-putrefaction. All better methods came in with the whites.

Notwithstanding the prodigality of nature and his independence of the cares which beset the modern man, the old Indian was not wasteful of his resources.

He picked no more berries than he needed to stay the cravings of his hunger, and scrupulously avoided injuring trees and bushes which bore anything edible. He killed no more game than he needed for himself and his camp, and ate every part of what he did kill. When he built a fire, he used only the fuel that was necessary, and before quitting the spot extinguished the flame with care.

Along came the white man, the finished product of centuries of civilization, and reversed nearly everything the Indian was doing. Is it strange that the Indian found him self-contradictory and incomprehensible? He professed to be the follower of a Prince of Peace, yet his distinguishing insignia were weapons for destroying life, and his manners were domineering and bristling with threats. He worshipped a Deity whom he professed to trust as an ever-provident Father, yet he was always taking thought for possible sufferings on the morrow, and stood ready to risk his life in storing up wealth which he could not use himself. He glorified ease, yet worked incessantly. He built a house with great labor, and divided it into rooms which would require him to move about, though pretending to associate rest and quiet with a home. Instead of mastering the several arts required to minister to his own wants, he delved incessantly at one employment to the disregard of others. He was a farmer or a blacksmith, a miner or a tailor, a soldier or a priest: and the soldier could not farm nor the priest weld metals. He was always decrying waste, yet threw away enough to subsist a fellow-man. If he hunted, his trail was strewn with untasted meats.

If he built a fire for a night's camp, it must be big enough to illuminate a whole canyon.

It has puzzled many observers of the Indian to make out where he draws the line of differentiation between the ideas of the white man which he adopts and those which he discards. It never seemed to me particularly mysterious: he simply accepts the things which penetrate his understanding and appeal to his common sense, and rejects the others. He makes his garments now of cloth, and exchanges his rawhide tepee for one of canvas or cotton sheeting, because game has become so scarce that he can no longer procure skins as of old. He eats flour, because it saves the women of his household the drudgery of grinding the grain between flat stones. If he wears a hat, it is not for the purpose of keeping his head warm, but because its broad brim will protect his eyes from the direct rays of the sun. He prefers a gun to his old bow and arrow, because it will bring down his game at longer range. He puts a bit into his pony's mouth and a saddle upon its back, or hitches a wagon behind it, because these accoutrements will help him to travel more easily.

But he does not take so kindly to the stiff leather shoes of the white man, accepting them only under protest, when it is inconvenient to get his yielding moccasins. A coat, with its refractory sleeves, he will not wear unless compelled to, though the white man's waistcoat, with its open armholes, resembles his ancestral hunting-shirt enough to win him to its use pretty promptly, while for an outside covering his blanket supplies all needs. If he is obliged to own a house, he would rather turn it over to his horses or utilize its waste space for storage purposes, and erect a canvas tepee or a brush wickiup in the yard for his own occupancy. He adopts the ready-made aniline dyes, because they give him the vivid reds, blues, and greens of which he is so fond, without the trouble of decocting the vegetable stains. He adorns his raiment with German beads, since porcupine-quills have become less abundant and the art of coloring them has so largely died out among his people. He even looks with favor on a parlor organ, because, though nobody in his family can play it, the children can amuse themselves by pressing bellows and keys and hearing the instrument wail as if it were a living thing; but the chances are that he will keep it outside of his house, where the rains and sand-storms work their will with it unhindered. And if his wife buys a sewing-machine because it will enable her to wear three times as many dresses as she can when she has to make them toilsomely with the common needle, neither she nor he will probably spend five minutes' thought on oiling its joints or replacing any part which has become useless through unskilful handling.

The casual traveler to-day through that part of the West which we long styled the frontier, will look in vain for the noble red men so romantically portrayed in Catlin's paintings and the moving-picture films. It is only by leaving the beaten paths of travel and wandering far afield that one comes into contact with interesting remnants of the ancient race, amid characteristic surroundings. Not many of the old-

style Indians are left, even there. As a rule, the
women are far more conservative than the men, but
both sexes have felt the effect of brushing elbows with
Caucasian civilization, however slightly.

Most of the men continue to wear their hair long,
and woven into two braids, which hang over their
shoulders in front; not a few paint their faces in part;
and their gaudy neckerchiefs, bead chains, big silver
rings and bracelets, and gold ear-pendants recall the
stage in the evolution of this people when, as in the
bird world, the forth-faring male monopolized the
bodily decorations, and left all soberer habiliments to
the female home-keeper, whose function it was to
watch over their growing family and keep everything
in order for his return. The women, save for the
better materials of which their clothes are made, present much the same outward appearance now that
they did in the days of the gold fever and the pony
express. But neither men nor women lead the same
lives or wear the same air that they did even as lately
as then. The men have largely lost their spirit, the
women their gayety. The advance of the new social
order into their country may have made existence
easier in some respects, but with it have come a distinct loss of self-dependence and certain forebodings
which have fallen like a chill upon hearts once care-
free.

These latter-day Indians are, for the most part,
dirty in their persons, habits, and homes. This was
to be expected, doubtless, in view of the particulars
in which their mode of life has been changed. The
rude cleansing which used to be done by the winds

sweeping through their camps, and by the natural evaporation of the moisture on skin exposed to the sun, no longer comes to pass now that they wear clothing which smothers the body, and sleep and eat in substantial houses. The Indian who has once been led to array himself in " citizen's dress," and huddle his family together in a building with solid sides, an immovable roof, and windows that can be closed without excluding the light, speedily yields to the enervating influence of such luxuries. He is apt to cover himself with the same weight of clothing in winter and summer, and wear these garments night and day. When the season of cold winds and snows begins, he proceeds to build the biggest fire his stove will hold, seal windows and doors hermetically, and pass his nights in the close atmosphere thus created, regardless of the fact that some members of his household may be suffering from diseases which thrive and spread in confinement.

He looks about him and sees children dying on every side. His older neighbors who used to be stalwart hunters or warriors have fallen into a state of lethargic indifference. He bewails the degeneracy of the young men who are coming to the front of affairs, making no claims to the prowess which was the chief pride of an earlier generation, but content if they can procure tobacco enough to keep a cigarette always alight, and coin enough in their pockets to give zest to a game of chance. Ask your old red man what all this means and he will tell you that it is the effect of the white man's intrusion into his country. It is the white man's wealth, the white man's power, the white man's cunning, and the white man's restless energy which have made the Indian—conscious of his inability to cope with the new conditions grafted upon his own simple environment in spite of his resistance—so hopeless and sodden.

Now leave the old man's camp and enter one of the pioneer white settlements, and you are impressed ere long by the discovery that there is another side to this picture. Here you find a few Indians living among the whites on terms of equality, class with class; for there is no such caste line, drawn on color, between the white and red races in the West as there is between the white and black races in the South. You will find neat Indian women holding their places as mistresses of white men's homes. You will be waited on, across the counter of the general store, by an Indian clerk. At the railway station you will find young Indian men trundling freight about the platform, and in the rural highways you will meet Indian teamsters hauling produce on the first stage of its journey from farm to market. You will see Indian harvesters in the grain fields, and Indian laborers digging a public irrigation canal. An Indian hostler will look after your horse at the livery stable.

When you have saturated yourself with these observations, have a chat with one of the hangers-on at your hotel: he will assure you that the Indian, wherever you find him, is lazy, morose, dishonest, a cumberer of the ground whose extermination would be a blessing to the community. Then talk to the best people you meet in the town, and they will tell you with equal positiveness that, though the Indian has faults and many of them, he is a good fellow at bottom, and everybody sympathizes with him as the under-dog in a long, hard, and bitter race conflict. And, to cap the climax of this bewildering farrago of phenomena and opinions, you learn from all sides that the educated Indian is the poorest specimen of his people, and the ignorant, non-progressive Indian the worthiest.

How shall we reconcile so many inconsistencies? By remembering, first, that it has been the fate of the red man, ever since he began to have white neighbors, to be judged, for public purposes, by persons whose range of vision is limited by their individual experience. Merchants who have sold goods to Indians on credit for many years, will bear as prompt witness to their honesty as swindlers who have tried to cheat them will bear to their trickiness. Soldiers who have had to do with them in frontier wars have told us that they are trusty allies and brave foes, while more than one historian of repute has accused them of an habitual treachery incompatible with any of the sterner human virtues. An employer who has used Indian labor for years testifies that when he sets a gang of red men at a job, he can go away and leave them without fear that they will stop work or shirk it as soon as he is out of sight; whereas one who has no idea of how to handle them is quite as positive that they cannot be depended on from hour to hour. The impatient white denounces the Indian as sullen, though one who meets him on a sympathetic footing finds him full of humor. White men who have made the acquaintance of the Indian only after he has been debauched by those who would rob him, regard him as a weak creature, who is naturally easy to victimize and therefore has never had half a chance; while those who have crossed weapons with him in a contest of shrewdness declare that he wears his appearance of unsophistication only as a mask. Rarely indeed has any white sociologist attempted to study the red race as a whole, on philosophic lines. Every one who does, reaches the conclusion that it is inherently little better or worse than any other race, and that many of the traits which are popularly regarded as typically Indian are in fact not natural racial peculiarities, but characteristic of primitive peoples in general, or the product of some special course of self-imposed discipline.

Still, all this fails to explain the almost universal disparagement, by the Western settler, of the educated by comparison with the uneducated Indian. At the outset, it is a question of terms. What his critics usually mean by an educated Indian is not one who has had his schooling at home, or one who has received a degree from a college of standing, but one who has been sent away to a big boarding-school a long distance from his reservation, and put through a five, six, or seven years' course of study. If he returns with an engraved certificate of proficiency, a starched collar, and patent-leather shoes, resolved to impress the world with his importance and use it as a lever for his own advantage rather than that of his people, he is at once accepted by the unthinking as an illustration of all that the white man's education does for an Indian. What happens?

He has so far forgotten his native tongue that he cannot converse in it with his family or former playmates. His parents look askance at his strange ways; to his brothers he is to all intents a foreigner. Where he had dreamed of an admiring welcome, he is met with only an incredulous or uncomprehending aloofness. He is loftily censorious of local conditions with which his long absence has put him out of touch, and the only person he can make a target for his complaints is the Superintendent of his reservation, with whom he is soon embroiled, and against whom he pours a flood of charges into Washington. The result of such a clash is almost surely defeat for the accuser, as the Agent has the ear of the government, while the returned student's standing is still dubious. Then he denounces everybody and everything connected with the Indian Service as corrupt, and lapses into petty mischief-making or utter idleness. Meanwhile, however, his too ready acceptance as a type has thrown into obscurity his worthier classmate, whose desire is to get once more into sympathetic relations with his people, and to help them by his unostentatious but wholesome example; who, if he cannot make a living at one calling, is ready to take up another, however humble; till presently he settles into his place as a member of the quiet, law-abiding element, of whom nobody inquires whether his intelligence was trained at home or abroad.

The question of how the red man ought to be educated has given rise to some of the warmest controversies ever waged over his treatment at the hands of our race. In the Colonial era, the chief concern of the civilized whites was for the Indians' conversion to Christianity, as is shown by endowments given to certain important seats of learning. Harvard University was chartered in 1650 for the " education of the English and Indian youth of this country in knowledge and godlynes," and its first brick dwelling was erected about 1660 for an Indian college. A generation later, William and Mary College set up an Indian department; and Dartmouth College was started as an institution for preparing Indian youth for missionary work among their own people. What is now Princeton University was long identified with a similar project. So little interest, however, was manifested by the Indians in these efforts in their behalf that one enterprise after another was abandoned, and finally the whole responsibility for the instruction of the Indians was transferred to the churches which maintained missions among them. Not till 1819 did the nation at large take any pronounced step toward the support of Indian schools.

From the small beginnings of that day, the Indian educational system has grown to such proportions that we now spend on it four million dollars a year and more. It embraces, in round numbers, twenty non-reservation boarding-schools, with an attendance of 7,600 pupils; seventy reservation boarding-schools, with 10,000 pupils; and one hundred and fifty day-schools, with an enrollment of 6,500. Besides these, all of which are secular, several of the religious denominations support schools on the reservations, where tenets of the Christian faith are taught in conjunction with the ordinary branches of learning, and the five tribes originally settled in Oklahoma have schools of their own. The larger government non-reservation schools carry their pupils through what we know as the eighth grade, and in a few cases do some high-school work and a little commercial training; and they are equipped with agricultural lands and dairies, and with shops in which rudimentary industrial instruction is given. The reservation boarding-schools are, in a way, reduced copies of the non-reservation schools, the scope of their technical instruction being much narrower, the scholastic course shorter, and the ages of the pupils generally somewhat younger.

Observe that both these classes of schools offer the Indian not only free tuition, but also free lodging, free food, free clothing, and free medical attendance, thus going several degrees farther than the most liberal provision anywhere made for the youth of other races at public expense, except in institutions for paupers, criminals, and defectives. Even the transportation of the pupils to and fro is paid for by the government. We find but one opinion now as to cutting off the free rations formerly doled out to the adult Indians on the reservations, because eating the bread of charity will sap the sturdiest human character; but is it any better to carry off the children indiscriminately, train them to despise practically all that their race stands for, and saturate them with the idea that, for whatever they wish, they have only to draw upon a rich and indulgent government? And, even putting the best face upon it, does the upbringing of an individual here and there mean the improvement of a race?

These comments will show why I have always believed that the key to the problem of Indian education lies not in establishing more of the big institutions, but in the multiplication of the little day-schools to which the children can come every morning and from which they can go home every night. In the family circle the children describe the day's happenings at school, and the parents absorb unconsciously some of the message the teacher is bringing from the outside world. The teacher, in turn, catches some of the atmosphere of the home from the children, and is able to do better work with them in consequence. Through the mutual understanding thus developed, an opening is made for the missionary; and when you have a whole camp or village subject to the leaven, it seems to me you are contributing to a scheme of race elevation on pretty broad lines.

Take still another view of the question. We gather a small army of children from camp and cabin, where all living is strictly from hand to mouth, and place them in a huge school which to their dazzled eyes seems like a town, and where mechanical devices supplant hand labor as far as practicable. As a precaution against fire the buildings are lighted by electricity instead of candles or lamps, so that whoever desires to illuminate a room can do so by merely pressing a button in the wall. In order to save time and energy where so many human beings are collected under one roof, the washing of clothes and bedding is done in a modern laundry. The entire premises are heated from a central plant, whence the warm air or steam is conducted through pipes to wherever it is wanted, and may be set free by the turning of a screw. The food is prepared in great cauldrons and bake-ovens connected with a mammoth range, or a series of ranges, fed with coal. Everything else that ministers to the needs of daily existence is done on a similar grand scale.

How far does all this go toward elevating the red race? How many of the children, whose whole conception of life outside of an Indian camp is founded on their experiences at such a school, will be fitted thereby to cope with the conditions amid which they will be thrown after graduation? Those who go back to their old homes will find nothing there corresponding to what they have had about them during their pupilage. Or, if they settle in some white community and try to earn their living in any of the pursuits open to them, how many will find themselves so situated that they can light their rooms by pressing a button or heat them by turning a screw, or cleanse their garments in a laundry started by a pull on a lever, or have their bodily comfort generally looked after by persons hired to take care of them?

" But," argues the advocate of the segregation system, "surely the pupil is led a little farther along the path of civilization by learning to wear a nightgown to bed, to sleep between sheets, and to eat his meals from a table with a knife and fork, instead of throwing himself on the ground at night and sleeping in the clothes he has worn all day, or maybe for many days, and clawing his food out of the common frying-pan with his fingers!" Undoubtedly. Still, he does not need a long separation from his home for that. In Red Man's Land, day-schools differ considerably from those in our populous centres. Besides the "three R's," most of them teach the girls such things as simple sewing, the rudiments of cookery, how to wash their clothes in a tub, how to make a bed and set a table. The boys are taught to raise a few vegetables, perhaps to take care of a cow or some pigs, to keep up a wood fire in a cookstove, to draw and carry water from a well, to make rude repairs with a hammer and nails, to sweep and dig and do other work which should fall to the stronger members of a household. Both sexes are drilled in the practice of bodily cleanliness, keeping their effects in order, and eating properly the little lunch which is set before them at noon. In short, what they learn at the day-school is a step above anything known at home, but only a step, easily mastered—not a sudden flight to heights hitherto undreamed of. Any one who is skeptical of the difference between the two methods of training, need only go into Red Man's Land and study their respective effects on the communities there.

But we must not lose sight of the fact that the Indians are rapidly becoming citizens, and as such are coming into relations with the public educational establishments of the states in which they reside. Several years ago a wise movement was begun, to encourage those Indians who lived near enough to any common school to send their children there instead of to a distinctively Indian school. I was able, while

OLD APACHE WOMAN.

in office, to carry this policy a stage farther, by opening Indian schools to white pupils—a privilege which
it seemed might be welcomed by settlers who had
taken up homesteads in a newly opened reservation.
The main object in both cases was the same—to bring
about the mingling of the two races in childhood, so
that as the young people grew up they would have
a more friendly feeling toward each other. The plan
has succeeded sporadically rather than uniformly. In
most neighborhoods with a mixed population the
whites have been glad to let Indian children attend
the public schools as long as the government would
pay the cost of their tuition. In others, white parents
have objected to letting Indian children mingle with
theirs, not on grounds of race prejudice, but because
the homes from which the little Indians come are so
often ill-kept, loosely disciplined, and unwholesome,
that infection is feared, moral as well as physical.
Again, not a few Indian parents have kept their children out of the common schools because, in their
ragged and unkempt condition, they have been made
butts for the ridicule of thoughtless white playmates.
These, however, are exceptions to a rule based generally on common sense.

The policy just described will, it is hoped, help
bridge the gap between the past centuries of racial
separation and the dawning era during which the
red man will take his place with the rest of us in
the body politic. Changed conditions in the Western country have convinced a majority of our people that the practice of the fathers, of keeping red
men and white as far as possible out of reach of each

other, was the worst sort of a makeshift, and we are reversing it as fast as we can. The army, for instance, which began by organizing separate Indian troops, now enlists Indians on the same footing and for the same service as whites, mixing them in the ranks. In the navy, Indian seamen are, as a rule, the most popular members of the crews to which they are attached. Indian athletes compete in the world's contests. Indian politicians can aspire to any office in the gift of their fellow-citizens without risking a rebuff on account of their blood.

More important than all, in the light of its ultimate benefit to the Indian, is his steadily increasing prominence in the Western labor markets as a fellow-worker and rival of the men of other races. Almost my first act as Commissioner, and the one in which I feel perhaps the greatest satisfaction, was the establishment of an employment agency, which should find jobs for Indian laborers and Indian laborers for jobs, outside of the reservations. Why " outside " is it asked? Because, to the Indians who have neither taste nor talent for farming, or who lack the land and implements and education necessary to follow that calling successfully, the reservations offer no incentives to industry, but every possible temptation to idleness and vice. On reservations where rations have been abolished, efforts have been made to invent some artificial pretence of work which the Indians can do, and thus go through the form of earning from the government the wages needed to buy their provender. But this is so hollow a mockery that the Indians see through it, and laugh among themselves at the stupidity of the whites in supposing that it deceives anybody. All the moral effect of industry is lost, of course, upon a man who realizes that the task he is set to perform is not productive labor, but a rather cheap means of cloaking charity in the guise of self-support.

IV

THE RED MAN AND OUR SOCIAL ORDER

I am getting old now, and I am getting up in years, and all I wish at the present time is for my children to grow up industrious and work, because they cannot get honor in war as I used to get it. They can get honor only by working hard. I cannot teach my children the way my father taught me, that the way to get honor is to go to war; but I can teach my children that the way to get honor is to go to work, and be good men and women.—CHIEF RUNNING BIRD, *of the Kiowas*.

It is often said that the Indian child, after receiving the best education that we can give, will return to barbarism at the first opportunity. It is a fact that some Indian children and youth do go back to the blanket and their wild life. How can they help it? . . . Those who have been most successful in civilizing Indians, brought about a gradual separation from savage ways of living, and introduced various peaceful industries among them. It was a necessity. There is no virtue which I have not seen exemplified in some of the different Indian tribes with which I have had to do. As a rule, they kept their promises to me with wonderful fidelity, often putting themselves to extraordinary exertion and peril.—GENERAL O. O. HOWARD.

IV

THE RED MAN AND OUR SOCIAL ORDER

WHAT we Caucasians call society is a very complex affair, and we cannot wonder that the Indian finds it so hard to understand. By way of a crude analogy, imagine a newsboy taken suddenly out of the streets and given a responsible position in a modern department store. You may reason that he has learned to buy his papers every day for one cent apiece and sell them for two cents, and that this embraces all the essential principles of trade; but of a thousand boys thus translated from their narrow sphere of direct activity to one involving the highest degree of organization, the most elaborate division of labor, the closest calculations, and the largest risks, how many do you believe would be able to cope with the multitude of new elements brought into their lives?

Now proceed a step further and suppose that, when your newsboy shrinks back appalled and declares that he would rather remain in his old business in spite of its hourly hardships and its insignificant rewards, you tell him that that is out of the question; that you know better than he does what will most promote his welfare; that what you are offering him is a great immediate boon, and a yet greater opportunity for himself and his posterity; that he ought to be devoutly thankful for such blessings; and that, whether he is or not, you are going to compel him to accept them: there you have the nearest conceivable parallel to the situation of the American Indian. Accustomed always, and descended from ancestors always accustomed, to a mode of living as simple as that of the patriarchs of ancient Israel, he is suddenly confronted with a social system too labyrinthine for his comprehension, and required to make himself a vital part of it. Let us see what this involves.

Even were we to waive entirely the moral aspects of the matter, like the degrading effect of substituting whim for purpose, and convenience for obligation, in regulating the relations of the sexes among his people, we still must recognize the necessity of making the Indian conform to our customs with regard to marriage and divorce in order to safeguard his property interests. No person has a right to bring children into the world and deliberately leave them helpless and dependent on the community; yet that is what happens if we make the marriage tie so easily soluble as to put it into the power of a fickle-minded parent to change domestic partners practically at will. In Red Man's Land I have had occasionally to straighten out tangles in the property claims of children of three or four successive marriages made by one man or one woman, or by a man and woman who, after starting a family, separated and took each a fresh partner or a series of partners. Such a task is hampered at every turn by the difference between the common law of descent among Indians and whites.

respectively.   It is almost the universal rule in Indian tribes that descent is traced through the mother, and this is undoubtedly the natural course, because there never need be any uncertainty as to who is the mother of a child; but the rule which is as nearly universal in Caucasian communities is the precise opposite of this.   Our departure from nature has its origin in our desire to fortify the popular ideals of family unity, the sanctity of marriage, and the purity of the home. By recognizing the father as the vehicle of descent, and, to that extent, of inheritance, we emphasize the material importance of assuring the chastity of the mother, which is one point gained for morality, at least.

The practice of polygamy among the Indians has never been so common as is generally supposed.   The broad rule of monogamy, subject to exception under certain conditions, was based wholly on economic considerations.   A very young man could scarcely hope to make such success in war, the chase, or pastoral pursuits as would warrant his trying to take care of more than one wife; so polygamy, where we have found it at all, has been confined almost entirely to the few older men who, having achieved prominence and a fair supply of worldly comforts, took pride in their excess of wives as an index of their prosperity, just as successful white men often parade their landed estates and their magnificent scale of living.

A far worse evil lies in promiscuity.   The polygamist who takes good care of three wives at once, and of all the children they bear him, is an exemplary member of society by contrast with the man who takes to himself three wives in rapid succession, casting off one without ceremony as soon as another attracts his fancy, and ignoring his obligations to the children of each from the moment he deserts her for her successor. Lately a campaign has been begun to break up the practice of fleeting marriages and indiscriminate dissolutions by requiring Indians, when they wish to be divorced, to resort to the processes prescribed by statute in the states of their residence. Even in those states where divorce is easiest, this requirement has the effect of warning the Indians that marriage and divorce are matters of too great consequence to depend on the impulse of the moment; and thus it lays in their minds the foundations of respect for law generally.

The cultivation of a higher esteem for the marriage bond has been helped in no small degree by a plan, instituted about the beginning of the present century, of keeping at every agency a system of family records for the Indians under its jurisdiction. This not only involves the careful entry of all births, deaths, and marriages as they occur, but an inquiry into the ancestry and collateral relationships of living Indians, as far as the facts are obtainable from the older people of the tribe. At first, the Indians were very wary of giving such information, not understanding why any one should ask for it, and suspecting that behind the whole business lurked another trick of the white people to take something away from them. They are responding more readily now.

A feature of our social order which the red man was most reluctant to adopt was that of land-ownership. Our idea of fencing in a certain portion of the soil and establishing an indefeasible claim to it which we can convey to a purchaser, or transmit to our individual posterity, was foreign to everything in his traditions. Although every tribe had its recognized territory to inhabit, land was, in the aboriginal view, one of those necessaries of life which, by virtue of their character, must always remain common property. Among the hunting tribes its chief use was to afford a range for the wild game animals; among the pastoral tribes it was valuable only as a place to graze sheep or cattle; while among the agricultural Indians of the Southwest it was parceled out periodically to those who would be sure to use it, or to the most active partisans of the element in power in the village government. I need not go again into the story of how we revolutionized everything in this domain; and, first by the purchase or conquest of successive tracts of territory, then by the reservation system, and finally by the allotment process, gradually forced the white custom of individual and complete land-ownership upon the native people.

A close kindred exists, of course, between our way of dealing with land, the most stable of all our forms of property, and our system of jurisprudence, the most stable of all our public institutions. So, after introducing into the newly opened country the idea of abstract landlord rights as distinguished from occupancy of the soil dependent on its utilization for subsistence purposes, the white colonists set up their courts of justice and transplanted here the great body of law and the fixed forms of procedure which their fathers had developed in the Old World as the fruit of centuries of struggle and study. To these, and to anything resembling them, the Indian was a total stranger. When he engaged in a dispute with a neighbor, if neither party was disposed to violence as a quick means of settling the issue, they referred the whole matter to a council of old and wise men, who heard them state their differences and then reached a decision after long and solemn deliberation. Nearly always the council advised a compromise, and the force of tribal opinion was so effective that the disputant would have been rash, indeed, who refused to carry it out in good faith. There were no written records, no citation of precedents other than tribal custom, no formulation of principles to govern similar cases for all time, no appeal to higher tribunals from adverse rulings. Whatever was done, was done for the conclusion of the present controversy and the satisfaction of the present parties, leaving the past undisturbed and the future to take care of itself.

As soon as the government began systematically to parcel out the land of the Indians, it was obliged to attach a permanent and practicable name to every Indian, whereby he could be identified on the rolls of his tribe and in the deeds issued to him. Such names as Big Thunder and Leaping Crow, for instance, could be utilized without change, but one like Pulls-the-Bear-into-the-Canyon was a different matter. Hence arose the grotesque array found on some of the rosters, where a Christopher Columbus, a George Washington, and an Abraham Lincoln stand side by side with a Yellow Cloud and an Omaha Jim.

Recent years have brought more sanity, and the rule is now to retain, wherever that is possible, at least a part of the Indian name borne by the tribesman among his own people.

In the matter of costume, I never could see why we should not allow the Indian the same latitude we grant to members of other races. If a white man preferred a suit of chain-armor to one of broadcloth, I suppose we should set it down to eccentricity, and think no more about it. Even on the score of modesty it is possible to draw distinctions more nice than logical. In an iron foundry, or the engine-hold of a steamship, we find men stripped to the waist, and at an athletic contest bare legs are the rule; yet our only comment is that the clothing—or the lack of it—in such cases is adapted to the work to be done. The swimmer crops his hair as short as he can, while the football-player cultivates a mop, and it does not occur to any of us to criticise the contrast, because each extreme has a purpose behind it. To the Indian, however, conventional observers concede no such range of liberty. If he wears his hair in long braids and discards a hat, or folds a blanket about him as a substitute for an overcoat, he is pronounced a savage without more ado, and every effort is made to change his habits in these regards.

Are we not thus attending too much to externals, at the risk of distracting attention proportionally from things of more vital importance to him? Wherever his attire conflicts with decency or health, we are bound to demand its discontinuance; but from that point onward, would it not be wiser to drop admonitions and trust to the lessons of experience? When he discovers that there are practical advantages in a well-scrubbed skin, that keeping his hair at easy combing length frequently relieves him of discomforts incidental to its neglect, and that a man who is sawing wood or guiding a plough has other uses for his hands than holding a blanket about him, the paint and the braids and the blanket will fall away of themselves, never to return.

The same is true of his mode of life generally. When we persuade him to live in a solid house instead of a tent, I am by no means sure that we are doing him a good turn. In spite of its being a symbol of permanency and thrift, his house increases his sensitiveness to cold, and discourages ventilation, leaving him more susceptible to tuberculosis. Also, his old practice of shifting his habitation from place to place whenever the ground around it became foul from accumulated refuse, was a fairly effective insurance against filth diseases, as shown by the fact that far worse epidemics have prevailed among tribes who lived in houses than among those whose shelters were readily removable.

A condition much more troublesome to handle has to do with dancing and kindred ceremonials. As we have seen, the dance began not as a recreation, but as a religious function. A war dance, for example, was conducted for the purpose of conciliating the divinities who presided over arms and bloodshed, so that the band performing the dance might be favored in battle and triumph over their enemies; a corn dance, or a harvest dance, was a special homage paid to the agricultural divinities who were expected to respond by increasing the fruits of the earth; and so on through the list. Now, no matter how earnestly one may desire to convince an Indian that he can accomplish nothing by such appeals, it is a waste of energy to try to reason out this conclusion by the usual processes of logic; and even after an Indian has embraced a more spiritual religion, his conservatism often will betray itself, if not in his secret participation in the old rites, at least in an attitude toward them which shows what a wrench it costs to tear himself free from the superstitions inherited from his ancestors, and instilled into him from babyhood by the elders of his tribe.

Unhappily, however sincere may have been the motives of their participants in the old days when a real importance was attached to the tribal dances, these have become, under modern conditions, among the strongest influences for race demoralization. The younger generation see in them nothing of their ancient significance, but only a colorful mummery, kept alive for tradition's sake. The white people in the neighborhood, drawn to the dances at first by curiosity, presently turned them to commercial account by advertising their attractions to visitors from afar, with the result which always follows making merchandise of a religious observance. As fast as their primitive dignity was wrung out of such ceremonials, vulgarity crowded into its place. Liquor began to be smuggled in to inflame the dancers and debauch the attendant Indians. The red women and girls naturally have been the chief sufferers from the change, till by degrees the camps surrounding some of the great dances have been converted into open markets of vice, with all that that description stands for.

It is the dancing habit, too, which most sadly interferes with the Indian's progress as an industrial worker. He will accept employment at good wages, where he has a fine outlook for increasing his skill and thereby improving his worldly condition; for a month or six weeks, perhaps, he will remain steadily at his job; but by that time, if he has accumulated a little money, the chances are that he will wish to go home to take part in a dance which is to be held at his camp on a day when the sun shall rise behind a certain notch in the eastern hills. I assume that eventually he will be educated to greater steadfastness in industry by the same hard experience which has taught the rest of us that if any will not work, neither shall he eat.

The dance has yet another serious aspect: it is one of the instrumentalities used by the medicine-man, or native healer, in the cure of disease; and until this superstition can be uprooted we cannot hope to make much headway with public sanitation among the Indians. In a case of individual illness, after the incantations of the medicine-man have failed to produce any effect, a sufferer will sometimes seek an educated physician, to see whether the " white man's medicine " may perchance have some merit when added to " Indian medicine." But public sanitation is a different thing; being preventive rather than curative, it touches a phase of the health question which is quite beyond the horizon of the Indian's observation. To his fatalistic mind it seems a useless expenditure of trouble to keep the camp and its inmates always clean as a precaution against epidemics: when an epidemic comes, as it is bound to from time to time, a big dance can be held to exorcise the demons that brought it on, and then all the survivors will be well and happy again! So the Indians in the camp continue to live as they have always lived, and allow their places of abode to become as dirty as they may; the victims of skin diseases pass them on to their well neighbors by sharing the same clothes, bedding, and domestic utensils; while tubercular patients spit recklessly in all directions.

Our race inherits in its blood a genius for organization and a respect for authority when it places the welfare of the community above the convenience of the individual; but the red men have always disregarded the regulations of the Indian Office designed to protect them from epidemics, and the inadequacy of the laws which make the office responsible for the well-being of the Indians but leave it powerless to compel submission to its orders must be blamed for the ravages of disease on the reservations. Till 1908, about the only attention Congress had given to Indian health conditions was represented by an annual appropriation of five thousand dollars for the suppression of smallpox outbreaks. As to everything else, the physicians connected with the several agencies, or those in private practice near by who were under contract with the government to answer calls from Indians, were left to handle whatever came along as best they might. During the winter of 1908-09, one

of our Supervisors, a woman who had made a special
study of such subjects, came on from Phœnix, Arizona, to tell me that the "sore eyes" so common
among Indians thereabout had been definitely diag-
nosed as trachoma. It had spread so through the
large government school at Phœnix that there was
some talk among the medical men of the town about
requiring the municipal authorities to proclaim a quar-
antine against the institution. Without a moment's
delay I took the Supervisor with me to the Capitol,
where we called on the chairmen of the two com-
mittees of Congress who had jurisdiction of Indian
affairs, and within an hour procured the promise of
an emergency appropriation of $12,000, immediately
available. With this money in hand, I set up a
trachoma hospital at the Phœnix school, open to the
Indians of the surrounding country, and made it a
training-place for our own agency physicians and
nurses, brought, a few at a time, from all parts of
the West. This was the first step in the aggressive
warfare the government is now waging against in-
fectious disorders among the Indians. Next, I began the reorganization of the medical branch of the
Indian Service, and opened sanitarium schools for
children physically unfit to attend those of the ordinary
sort.

Home life like that which with us lies at the core
of everything social, is practically unknown among
the Indians in their primitive state. They live together in families, it is true, all the members of a
family sharing its dwelling. They meet in one place
to eat and drink and sleep, to make their garments

and prepare their weapons; but of the subtler kind of enjoyment which the Caucasian finds in his home, and which distinguishes that home from a mere enclosure for shelter, the Indian is ignorant. In his crude way he extends hospitality to his guests; but its scope is confined to laying before them food to satisfy their hunger and assigning them space in which to roll themselves in their blankets and stretch out their bodies for the night. Social intercourse commonly consists of spreading a feast and exchanging stories of prowess in hunting or in the presence of an enemy. Until a spirit of emulation was stirred among the Indian women by the missionaries and the government matrons, there was none of the pride of good housekeeping which we find among even the humblest white wives and mothers.

A great deal has been accomplished in this direction by the tribal fairs which have been held for several years now in certain reservations. At these shows, the competition is keen not only among the Indians who farm and who struggle to produce the largest ears of corn, the heaviest potatoes and beets and melons, but also among the women, who contest for prizes offered for the neatest tepee, the most palatable cookery, the best appointed dinner-table, and the most sensibly dressed children. In their wholesome rivalry we can detect the initial glimmerings of a home-making ideal like that which we find among the best women of our own race.

If we tried to put into one phrase a description of the Indians' social system, we should have to call it a patriarchal communism. The patriarchal basis underlies everything; and while there may not be, strictly speaking, a common ownership of property, yet the necessaries of life are so far recognized as for the common use that pauperism, as we know it, is not found among the Indians when left to themselves. The hungry man does not beg for food: he takes it wherever he sees it in the open. By this I do not mean that there is no such thing as a difference of worldly estate among these primitive people. On the contrary, there are gradations of prosperity among them as among us; only, wealth is measured among them by other standards than ours. One Indian family has more ponies, more cattle, more sheep, more blankets, more weapons, more ornaments than another; but if a famine season comes on, the cattle and sheep and ponies of the rich man are slaughtered, not to keep their owner strong and well while his less favored neighbor starves to death, but to subsist all who need food. And, in general, the Indian's ambition to be famous among his people as a free-handed friend leads him often to distribute all his most valued possessions among his fellow-tribesmen as gifts, though he may himself suffer sadly in consequence.

At the foundation of what we Caucasians call thrift is the disposition to accumulate. Nor can we disguise the fact that thrift is with us not merely a proper desire to provide against to-morrow's exigencies, but a craving to continue increasing the store so that one day we may cease striving altogether, live at ease ourselves, and hand down to our heirs the means of passing luxurious lives unembarrassed

NAVAJO CAMP SCENE.

by a sense of disastrous possibilities. To this aspiration the Indian is a stranger till we introduce him to it as a forward step in his social education. In his eyes, money has no value other than as a medium for procuring something he wishes. That procured with a part of his cash in hand, why hold on to the rest?

To him, too, next week is as good as this week for anything he wishes to do. It is his daily marvel why white men take so much trouble to live: is time about to come to a dead stop, that we must hurry so, and count the minutes, and postpone our rest and comfort till a future period when we shall be too old and feeble to enjoy them? Alas! deplore it though we may, we know that we must either keep pace with our generation, or fall by the wayside with the likelihood of being trodden under foot; and into this whirl we are forced to bring the Indian, no matter how little he or we may desire it. The situation is one not of preference, but of vital necessity. It is a waste of strength to declaim against evolutionary forces which are far stronger than any human instrumentality designed for their control: the only thing we can do is to accept the inevitable, and fortify the Indian to cope with it. In this brotherly aid lies his sole hope for the future.

V

ABORIGINES WHO ARE NOT RED MEN

Ice-built, ice-bound, and sea-bounded!
  Such cold seas of silence! Such room!
Such snow-light! Such sea-light confounded
  With thunder that smites as a doom!
Such grandeur, such glory, such gloom!
                    —JOAQUIN MILLER.

One of our most devoted and honored Home Missionaries, Dr. Sheldon Jackson, saw in the Russian reindeer an improvement upon the Alaskan dog travel, and the full answer to the Alaskan's isolation and hunger and destitution. It meant endurance and development of the Alaskan in the face of indifference, jeers, and hostile attacks, and at personal sacrifice he imported the reindeer and at last confirmed him as the exact need and promise for that country.

We hear a good deal about the Alaskan reindeer to-day, and we shall hear more to-morrow. The politician is as eager now to claim as he was before to repudiate and hinder. Do not let it be forgotten that this advance in civilization is due not to the politician, but to a missionary.—DR. WALLACE RADCLIFFE.

V

ABORIGINES WHO ARE NOT RED MEN

IT will surprise many readers, doubtless, to learn
that we have aborigines in the United States who
are not red men. Our federal statutes observe
the distinction by uniformly referring to them as
"natives," or, where some sweeping provision of
law regarding the Indians is intended for application
to all aborigines alike, emphasizing the fact. With
this preliminary understanding, it will seem less extraordinary that the expected people have never been
placed under the guardianship of the Office of Indian Affairs. They are in charge of the Bureau of
Education, which, very appropriately, has made the
school system the centre of its activities among them.

I am alluding now to a large proportion of the
native inhabitants of Alaska. We did not acquire
that province from Russia till 1867, and then we
bought it, so to speak, with our eyes shut. We had
only the vaguest notions about its climate, soil, resources, or population, but assumed on general principles that it was a land of perpetual snows, inhabited
by wild men who lived in huts built of ice-cakes and
subsisted on walrus and seal and polar bears' meat.
Even the boundaries were so uncertain that it took
more than thirty years to straighten some of them

out; and then we found that this little-known region was as large as the combined states of California, Oregon, Washington, Idaho, Montana, and New York, or, in other words, one-fifth the size of all the rest of the United States. It was discovered, also, that instead of annexing a single race of alien people, we had taken two or three races. Of these, however, the most distinctive type is found in the Eskimos, who by inter-marriage, trading, and other modes of affiliation, have stamped their neighbors with so many of their surface traits that the ordinary unscientific traveler is scarcely conscious of any differences.

The Eskimos often are spoken of as dwarfish in stature; as a matter of fact, there are many men among them of giant build, and the rank and file are of medium height, averaging perhaps five feet and four inches. Their clothing, which is made chiefly of the skins of wild beasts dressed with the fur on, and the muscular development of their shoulders due to the use of the paddle for propelling their boats, probably led to the common error by exaggerating their general breadth of body. They are of a light brownish-yellow color, with a pink tint on the more prominent features like the cheeks and lips. They have high heads, faces very wide across at the eye-line, bridgeless noses which are rather narrow except at the nostrils, and eyes of the general shape which we associate with the Mongolians of Asia. Despite their small hands and feet, they possess wonderful strength and endurance, the women carrying enormous loads without discomfort, and the men being able to make occasional journeys of fifty or seventy-five miles on foot without stopping to sleep. They are good-humored, with a considerable degree of natural intelligence, and, until corrupted by foreign influences, truthful in their statements. While their moral code takes little note of honesty in dealing with the property of others, the scamp detected in helping himself to the seal-meat or venison which a neighbor has hidden in the ice for future consumption may be killed by his victim without compunction. They will cheat in a bargain with the whites if they see the chance, yet theft as a trade seems to be practically unknown among them, as is also robbery with violence. Indeed, much of their dishonesty takes forms which enable them to laugh it off afterward as a bit of practical joking, and their love of fun is keen enough to give relish to a trick even when turned upon themselves. They are hospitable in the extreme, and polite to the point of going out of their way to avoid a speech, or act, which might wound the feelings of a stranger. These qualities do not prevent their being very sensitive to ill-treatment, and quite satisfied of their superiority to the mass of the white men who visit their country. Nor must it be inferred that their mild manners mean any lack of warlike spirit when aroused. On the contrary, if a quarrel is forced upon them, they show the courage which might be expected of a people accustomed to capture whales and fight bears for a livelihood.

In the relations of the sexes among themselves, those Eskimos who still remain in their primitive condition are almost lawless. Whether a man shall take one wife or many, or whether a woman shall have several husbands, seems to depend more on the numerical proportion of men to women in a settlement than on any other question. Women are bought and sold as chattels, and now and then are exchanged between husbands after marriage. There is no wedding ceremony beyond the mere act of taking. A wife being valuable chiefly for what she can be made to do for the comfort of the family—like drying, storing, and cooking the food, making and mending the clothes, and repairing the boats—her infidelities are disregarded except as they may interfere with the performance of her duties; but prostitution for gain did not exist among the Eskimos until the white whalers began to mix with them.

As the natives have no uniform means of reckoning time, it is hard to say at what age the women usually marry, but apparently they do not, as a rule, begin bearing children before they are twenty years old. A great many marriages are childless, and the smallness of the families into which children do come points to the conclusion that the race is on the decline. The death-rate is, of course, much enhanced by the ignorance of the parents as to providing properly for their little ones, and by the hardships of the life led by all. A family in which there are children makes much of them. They are nursed till three or four years of age, probably because the parents realize that the purely animal diet on which adults subsist would be injurious to infants. A mother carries her babe about with her, huddled in a little naked heap inside of the loose clothing on her back, and held in its place by her girdle, which for this purpose she wears a trifle higher than usual. At intervals she loosens the girdle, and shifts the babe around to her breast without exposing it to the air. After the child has become old and strong enough to walk alone, it often rides about on her back, with its legs straddling her body and passing under her arms—pick-a-back, as we should style it. A woman goes on with her accustomed work even with a pretty heavy child hanging to her in this way, and apparently is not much incommoded by her burden.

The older children relieve their mother by taking care of the younger ones, who seldom quarrel or cry, and who, in the absence of definite instruction, pick up whatever they know of life from observation and imitation. At seven years a normal boy will have learned how to use a small bow and arrow, and where and how to hunt for birds' eggs. At twice that age it is common to give him a gun and a seal-spear, and let him accompany the men in quest of large game. Lads of fourteen or fifteen sometimes will be found regular members of a whaling crew.

Like the Indians, many of the Eskimos take readily to mechanical pursuits, the necessity for making their own tools and weapons having sharpened in them the constructive and inventive faculties. They have also a decided artistic bent, which finds expression in carving. The tools they used for mechanical and artistic work were, until the whites introduced iron and steel among them, made chiefly of bone; and of this are still made, wholly or in part, many needles, thimbles, boxes, weaving devices, fish-hooks, seal-nets, harpoons, boat-bailers, crutches, adzes, mattocks, picks, shovels, saws, ice-scoops, skin-scrapers, flasks, pipes, drumsticks, and implements of nearly all other kinds employed by them. Some of the toys fashioned for the children are very ingenious. One is a manikin, with arms of whalebone so arranged that when they are pressed in a certain way he beats a drum held in his left hand with a stick held in his right. Another is a man in a kaiak, or canoe, which is worked by strings of cured animal sinew, so that he will make a stroke with his paddle and then recover, turning his head from side to side with each movement. There are whirligigs, teetotums, buzz-toys, pebble-snappers, and similar contrivances in profusion. Little girls among the Eskimos do not seem to care much for dolls, but they take kindly to skipping rope, and " play house " by arranging sticks on the ground as if for the boundaries of a dwelling and placing one of their number inside; the game being for the rest to try to invade the house and for the housekeeper to catch them while their feet are within its walls. Children of both sexes also play football with snowballs, and imitate the dancing of their elders.

Tobacco and alcohol were among the novelties to which the Eskimos were introduced by their early white visitors. In tobacco they have a discriminating taste, rejecting the cheaper and ranker mixtures when they can obtain a better quality even at a considerably higher price. So general has the use of tobacco become among them that unweaned babes are sometimes seen holding it in their mouths and swallowing the juice with no signs of nausea. As between the various forms of alcohol, the Eskimo's sole thought is to get that which will most readily effect intoxication. Indeed, whatever will accomplish this end is acceptable, whether it be whiskey or stale remnants of patent medicines and flavoring extracts.

With the Eskimos, as with the red men, the chief hope of the race lies in the training of the children, the adults being past the possibility of changing a great deal, though the adult Eskimo is far more susceptible to outside influence than the adult Indian. The Eskimo children are naturally bright. Their mental processes are stimulated, moreover, by their being thrown upon their own resources at a pretty early age, at least as to taking care of themselves in trading. A teacher in charge of one of the Arctic schools describes an illustrative incident. A year or two ago there sailed into the local harbor, just before the close of navigation, a whaling schooner manned mainly by Siberians. One evening after school about a dozen pupils, ranging in age from nine to fourteen, launched a canoe and went out to the ship, where they fell to bartering with the sailors. Before they came ashore they had traded away nearly everything they owned, some of them disposing thus of even their hats, caps, coats, suspenders, shirts, underwear, and pocketknives. On their return to the school they were overflowing with talk about their visit, and exhibited their trophies with much pride, for they had driven sharp bargains and brought back more value than they had let go, and they knew it without their teacher telling them.

Recognizing the commercial instinct as a powerful lever for civilization if well directed, and glad to encourage its cultivation among the young, several of the government schools are using it as the basis of their scheme of instruction. Arithmetic, for example, is made a conspicuous feature, daily drills being given in mental work and rapid calculation, and large use being made of problems in which the familiar commodities figure, so that the children will recognize the immediate practical bearing of everything they learn. Much emphasis is laid on oral English, also, in which the chief difficulty lies not in teaching the children the language, but in overcoming their timidity about attempting to speak it.

The head of one of the coast schools, a year or two ago, went a step further than most of his colleagues, and introduced a modified system of pupil self-government. The various duties involved in running the school he distributed among a series of offices, and then held an election to fill these offices. There was chosen a bell-ringer whose task it should be to sound the summons for the children for every session. Another functionary elected was a janitor who was made responsible for the tidiness of the schoolhouse; he was to appoint daily a staff of sweepers, and supervise their work while they cleaned the floors, dusted the desks and windows, and set the furniture in the right positions. Another was a librarian into whose custody was put all the books; he was to keep a written list of them, with memoranda of the shelves on which they belonged, and to enter the titles of those lent out and the names of the borrowers. A fourth was a stationer whose duty was to take care of the pens and pencils, paper and erasers, and attend to their circulation when needed. A fireman was charged with the building of the fires, and the study of the thermometer to make sure of a proper temperature in the schoolroom; chalk and ink inspectors doled out those necessaries to the pupils who had to work with them; a monitor kept a roll-book which contained the records of attendance, absence, and tardiness; a carpenter had the care of the tools, and was to report regularly on their condition; and so on. Above all these was placed a committee who kept an eye on matters generally, imposing fines for waste, carelessness, and other shortcomings serious enough to call for discipline.

This system, strangely enough, had its origin in a school so remote from civilization that it is cut off from all communication with the outside world, except for the visit of a government ship once a year in the summer. Yet the children seemed to take to it with as much avidity as if they had grown up in constant touch with the town-meeting and the popular primary. Under the encouragement of the Commissioner of Education, who is deeply interested in the experiment, it is spreading to the other schools all over Alaska.

Practical applications accompany all instruction. The advanced arithmetic classes, for instance, are put through a course in making out bills for the building materials entering into the construction of a schoolhouse. The lumber, nails, paper, shingles, and windows are figured at the prices prevailing in the larger American markets, and the children have these concrete examples to work on instead of the abstractions usually printed in the text-books. Then the food supply for a year is estimated and billed for purchase in the same way. A special touch of realism is given to the business by reckoning payments in furs and whalebone, supposed to be turned over in barter at the valuations commonly set upon these articles in the trade of the neighborhood. Lately an effort has been made to extend the influence of the schools, and further assure the natives of their usefulness, by inviting the older people to bring in their hides, ivory, etc., which they are going to send away to exchange for subsistence stores for their families. Their wares can thus be correctly counted and weighed, and packed and marked in a businesslike way for shipment, the invoices being made out just as in a city warehouse, and the commodities obtained in exchange being sent back to the shipper addressed in his own name. A surprising development, by the way, of the government's effort to provide better markets for the native products has been brought about by the extension of the parcel-post to this far-away region. In the old times, the natives were so often obliged to deal with the local traders exclusively that they had to be content with insignificant prices and were constantly in debt. But now they can send their furs and ivory through the mails to responsible commission merchants in Seattle, with the result that in some cases they command prices seventeen times as high as those they obtained before for goods of the same grade.

In the Aleutian Islands, which stretch in a curved

line from the toe of the Alaska Peninsula well over
the North Pacific Ocean toward the coast of Kam-
chatka, are found a group of natives who differ in
some particulars from the Eskimos, yet who are too
closely related to them for distinction in the popular
mind. Such differences as are most observable are
supposed to be due to their isolation from the main
body of their people, and their association with the
Russian adventurers who came in about the middle
of the eighteenth century and conquered them. Thus
Russian habits, and words from the Russian language,
were in course of time adopted by the Aleuts and
woven in with their own, till there was little of the
unadulterated native life left. Indeed, the name
Aleut, which the islanders have now firmly fixed upon
them, was not theirs originally : they used to call themselves Unungan. Whence they obtained their present
designation has long been a subject of dispute. At
one period it was assumed to have been derived from
a Russian word signifying a bold rock, and to have
referred to a geologic feature of some of the islands;
but most of the scientists I have heard discuss the
question recently think that the Russian discoverers,
mistaking these islanders for another group in whose
tongue " aliat " means " island," applied to them a corrupted form of this term, and thus Aliat, Aliut, or
Aleut was fastened to them, just as a geographical
error of Columbus when he discovered the West In-
dies was perpetuated in the name " Indian," by which
the aboriginal race in the body of our continent is
known.

The Aleuts have had a history more tragic in some

of its aspects, though less picturesque, than the history of the red man in the United States. Nature had been far from kind to them before they ever saw the face of a white man; and they appear to have been treated with such cruelty by the Russian traders who first settled among them that, after some years of this contact, their numbers had dwindled to less than one-tenth of what they were before the discovery. The abuses finally reached a point where the Russian government, prompted partly by a desire to establish a commercial monopoly, and partly, doubtless, by humanity, interfered and instituted measures for regulating the intercourse beween the two races. About this time, also, the missionaries began work, with the result of greatly improving the condition of the Aleuts, though not all the evils were eliminated. The population of the islands has increased and decreased by turns since these ameliorating influences became operative, epidemic diseases and a craving for intoxicants having played no insignificant part in its declines. It is now about eleven hundred.

A people naturally of high spirit, the Aleuts were disposed to hold their ground against the first advance of the Russians; but, with only their home-made darts to oppose to European firearms, their resistance was a pitiful failure, and the invaders soon reduced them to a condition of virtual slavery. From that day all their mettle seems to have gone out of them; they are quiet and teachable, but their docility is that of conscious and hopeless weakness. They continue at their old occupations of seal and otter hunting; and it must regretfully be admitted that for a number of years

ALASKAN TOTEM POLE.

after the islands had passed under the jurisdiction of the United States, the class of Americans who visited them carried in quite as many of the vices as of the virtues of Caucasian civilization, and in some instances threatened to parallel the bad record of their foreign predecessors.

Besides the Eskimos and the Aleuts, we find in Alaska the Athapascans, who live in the Yukon Valley and the smaller valleys that run into it. They are believed to be of Asiatic origin, but are so closely related in their habits to the red men of the United States proper as to call for only passing mention here. In southeastern Alaska, also, there are the Thlingits, who resemble the Athapascans except in language, and who have been so long in constant contact with the whites as to have lost a great many of their original characteristics and adopted the main features of our mode of living. They are a fine people, and it is gratifying to learn that their decline in numbers, which for seventy years under foreign domination proceeded at an appalling rate, appears to have been checked.

What can be done with natives of this sort is demonstrated by the experience of the Rev. William Duncan, who organized the Metlakatla colony which now has its home on Annette Island, near the southernmost extremity of the Alaska coast-line. Here is a community of between six and seven hundred souls, in which the manufacturing of commercial lumber and the canning of seafood, together with several minor industries and arts, are carried on with excellent effect. It must be borne in mind, however, in estimating the success of this enterprise, that one of its chief factors has been the barring of Annette Island from invasion by white miners. About fifteen years ago, some prospectors believed that they had discovered traces of valuable mineral deposits there, and tried to obtain permission from the United States Government to file claims and explore the leads; but Mr. Duncan visited Washington, and, presenting his protest in person and enlisting the aid of many influential men and women, managed to stave off what he regarded as the evil day for Metlakatla. Although the mining parties were excluded for the time being, it is inevitable that, if their belief in the mineral wealth of the island is well founded, they will renew their efforts sooner or later, and will win the right to enter and develop mines. Then will come the real test of the hold Mr. Duncan's teachings have upon his colony of natives. If their characters have been sufficiently strengthened to withstand the influences of compulsory association with the white element which always follows in the wake of a new mining venture, his work must be esteemed a triumph indeed, and the principle of prolonged seclusion on which it has rested will gain strength accordingly. Quite apart from its missionary appeal, the Metlakatla experiment has been, and will be, a most interesting sociological study.

The climate of a large part of Alaska is accountable for the slowness of its general development. In the regions bordering on the Arctic Ocean and Bering Sea, a fair midwinter temperature is 40 degrees below zero, and in spots it has fallen to 55°; while in the interior it has been known to go as low as 80°. When we consider what this fierce cold means in connection with six months of only briefly interrupted darkness, and that dependence for all communication with the outside world must be on ships which take their chances in an ice-laden sea, and on dog-sled trains at very irregular intervals, we can begin to appreciate the courage and fortitude of the pioneers of civilization in that part of the world.

More credit than is commonly accorded is due to the reindeer policy which the late Dr. Sheldon Jackson induced the United States Government to adopt in Alaska. It came about through the discovery, in 1890, of some Eskimo villages where a bad fishing season had reduced the inhabitants to the verge of starvation. Yet in northeastern Asia, only a few hundred miles away and subject to similar natural conditions, a large population were subsisting in comparative comfort by the use of the domesticated reindeer; for these animals, while living, furnished them with milk and pulled their sledges about, and, when killed, supplied nutritious meat, and hides which could be utilized for clothing, bedding, and wall and room coverings for their houses. The thought thereupon suggested itself to Dr. Jackson that if a lot of tame reindeer could be imported, and the Eskimos taught how to take care of them, a great problem might be solved almost automatically. It took Congress some years to assimilate this idea sufficiently to vote the money needed, but when it came to grasp the importance of the proposition it responded with a series of annual appropriations ranging from $5,000 to $25,000, and the work was launched.

The difficulties besetting a commerce in reindeer carried on between the Asiatic and American coasts were not confined to the handling of the animals with the indifferent equipment at command, or the perils of their transportation in vessels never designed for such purposes, but included the adjustment of satisfactory relations between the government and the missionary societies maintaining stations in Alaska. Theoretically, the government has no administrative connection with religious bodies of any name; but actually, in its undertakings in uncivilized regions, it has to depend a great deal on their friendly coöperation. In the reindeer enterprise this was markedly the case. The government fixed on a plan for distributing the animals, which began with the loan of herds, embracing each twenty-five males and seventy-five females, to mission stations for five-year periods, a station thus favored entering into obligation to educate a certain number of native apprentices in herdsmanship. At the end of the contract period the mission was to return to the government twenty-five male and seventy-five female deer of a younger generation, retaining whatever of the parent stock survived, and also the rest of the increase.

As the government schools multiplied through the wilder parts of the territory, they gradually took over the reindeer business from the missionaries, till now only a few of the mission stations retain their connection with it. The work has been steadily made more and more systematic. Under regulations approved by the Secretary of the Interior in 1907, an apprentice is allowed four years to learn his trade;

if he does well, he receives at the close of his first year six animals for his own, the next year eight, and the last two years ten each. Meanwhile, he is encouraged to go into freighting with his sled-deer, and by permission of his Superintendent he may kill his surplus stock from time to time and sell the meat and hides for his personal profit. On his graduation he becomes a full-fledged and independent herder, with his earnings for his capital, his accumulated deer for his first outfit, and some knowledge of business methods gained from his experience in transporting mails, passengers, and goods. He is still required, however, to conform to the rules of the reindeer service, which include a strict prohibition upon the sale of any female except to the government or to some other native designated by the government. The purpose of this restriction is to confine the benefits of the reindeer business to the people for whose sake the government embarked in it, and to prevent its drifting into the hands of the whites till the natives are everywhere well supplied and well instructed and the industry has become self-supporting.

The records show that the total number of reindeer in Alaska doubles every four years. If this rate of increase continues, there should be 150,000 head in the territory by 1920. Persons familiar with this region have figured out that there is enough land suitable for grazing, but fit for little else, to support four million deer, of which it would be safe to slaughter about one million every year, and ship the meat to the states; and not a few economic experts are considering the possibility that Alaskan reindeer-farming, which started as a pure benevolence, may yet help solve the riddle of a food supply for the children and grandchildren of our generation, not merely in the Arctic zone but everywhere in the country.

When the Russians came into Alaska, a good many unions were formed between Russian men and native women, and several of their mixed-blood descendants have risen to positions of prominence in their respective communities. The Russian law of the *" zemlia,"* which attaches the subject of the Czar to the soil of his domicile, came into strange operation here; for an employee of a Russian trading company, after serving his contract term in Alaska, was obliged to return to his home in the old country, whereas the woman who had cast her lot with him, no matter how fond they might be of each other or how faithful to their bond, had to stay in Alaska, because that was her home, and she could not be taken away from it, even to follow her partner. The fact, however, that such a separation was a matter of law and not of inclination, gave to the unions of whites and natives, entered into and maintained in good faith on both sides, the moral effect of marriage without its sacramental or statutory liabilities, so that no social ignominy attached to the parties where the whites and their domestic customs were dominant. The anomalous situation was changed when the United States took possession of Alaska, as the treaty of cession made it possible for any Russian subject resident there, should he so desire, to remain and become an American citizen; and the formal sanction of the law was extended to any union he might have formed with a native woman.

The Alaska natives number only about 28,000, less than one-tenth the Indian population of the United States. Thus far their case has presented few of the problems which have vexed the government for so many years in regard to the Indians. The situation in the territory more resembles that which grew out of our acquisition of the Philippine Islands from Spain. Alaska is separated by a considerable space from the main body of our republic. Large parts of it are still unknown except to scientific explorers, government officers, adventurers, and parties drawn thither for purposes of trade. The aborigines are of various degrees of social backwardness, and so distributed that they could array no force at any given point to obstruct the advance of the white race and its civilization. The land question there amounts to little, since the climate constricts agriculture within very close bounds, and only the minerals, the fur industry, and the fisheries offer any attraction to colonists from without. Moreover, starting with the idea that the country was purchased outright from its former owner, our government has never resorted to treaty-making with the native occupants, and has had no such technical compunctions to wrestle with in taking possession of whatever it wished, as it had when it helped itself to the property of the red men west of the Mississippi. It is safe to predict that there will never be any reservations in Alaska where the natives will be herded and fed and pauperized, or any allotment of farms with the notion of civilizing

them through the tillage of the soil. But one day—
and let the younger generation who read this prophecy
mark it for future reference—there will come a clash
between the natives and the whites over the fisheries.
When the full value of these is realized, the whites
will insist on regulating them by law; and the natives, owing to their lack of acquaintance with such
methods, will fail to get their fair share of the privileges dispensed by lease, license, or otherwise. They
will undergo a deal of trouble from punishment as
poachers, just as has happened on the coasts farther
south, and in the forests of the interior where rigid
game laws have superseded the old practice of unre-
stricted killing of wild animals for food.

VI

THE RED MAN AS TEACHER AND LEARNER

In all cases where it is possible we hope to keep for the Indian and for us what was best in his old culture. The Indians themselves must be used in such education; many of their old men can speak as sincerely, as fervently, and as eloquently of duty as any white teacher, and these old men are the very teachers best fitted to perpetuate the Indian poetry and music. The effort should be to develop the existing art—whether in silver-making, pottery-making, blanket and basket-weaving, or lace-knitting—and not to replace it by servile and mechanical copying. This is only to apply to the Indian a principle which ought to be recognized among all our people; a great art must be living, must spring from the soul of the people; if it represents merely a copying, an imitation, and if it is confined to a small caste, it cannot be great. . . .

The majority must change gradually, and it will take generations to make the change complete. Help them to make it in such fashion that when the change is accomplished we shall find that the original and valuable elements in the Indian culture have been retained, so that the new citizens come with full hands into the great field of American life, and contribute to that life something of marked value to all of us, something which it would be a misfortune to all of us to have destroyed.— THEODORE ROOSEVELT, in *The Outlook*.

VI

THE RED MAN AS TEACHER AND LEARNER

THE Caucasian race is convinced that it is the greatest on earth, and with reason. But some of us go a step further, and assume that our superiority to the other races means that we can learn nothing from them. This is a sad mistake, and nowhere worse than when we contrast ourselves with the American aborigines. Though we can teach them an immense amount about social organization, economy and efficiency in production, the preservation of health and the promotion of comfort, they in their turn can teach us many things by example.

Take, for instance, the matter of mental poise. The red man has a mind not proof against excitement, as is shown by some of his ceremonial performances in which he works it into a frenzy. These occasions, however, are sporadic. In his regular daily intercourse the Indian is calm, thoughtful, deliberate, contemptuous of turbulence in others. Speaking only when he has something to say, he speaks then with a candor which is refreshing, albeit startling at times. When one Indian thinks another a liar or a thief, he says so; it does not occur to him to hunt through his limited vocabulary for a euphemism which will convey an impression of his opinion without stating

127

it outright.   The Indian accused receives the charge
in a corresponding spirit.   If he is innocent, he says
so, and perhaps cites some incident in proof, but
he does not feel called upon to knock the accuser down.
The white man's quick and violent resentment in such
a case springs from the theory that his honor is his
most precious possession, which he can protect only
by punishing instantly any slur cast upon it.   And yet
the logic of the argument is with the Indian, who reasons that the blow does not establish the falseness of
the statement which called it forth; and he marvels
especially when he sees a white man exploding with
wrath over an imputation that one of his careless re-
marks is untrue, yet smirking with gratified vanity
at a hint that he has committed offences against the
moral law which by comparison make an indiscretion
of the lips seem trivial indeed.

Besides, whoever is well acquainted with the old-
fashioned Indian knows that he is as jealous of his
honor as the most high-minded Caucasian.   If he
gives you his word that he will do a thing, you may
safely stake your all on his fulfilment of his promise.   Repeatedly I have lent an Indian money in some
emergency, not seen him again for years, and then
had him hunt me up to lay before me the exact amount,
as if the loan had been made an hour before.   The
court records of the West teem with instances where
Indians indicted for the most serious crimes have been
allowed to go their way without a bond, on promising to appear on a given date for trial; and I have
yet to hear of one thus privileged who has broken

his pledge. That is the sort of honor which does not need bloodshed to vindicate it.

The calmness of the Indian appears nowhere to better advantage than in his treatment of his children. He does not find it necessary to storm at them in order to assert his authority. They are free to do pretty nearly anything they wish, and perhaps for that reason they are about as well-behaved as any in the world, for there is nothing in their discipline to arouse in them a spirit of resistance. And the interesting fact is plain to all students of the Indian that as these children grow up they have a reverence for their elders which is seldom found nowadays among ours. It might not be practicable for us to imitate in its extremes the aboriginal model of family training; but the self-control shown by the Indian parent in his avoidance of noisy rebukes and intemperate forms of expression, and his general indisposition to carp on petty annoyances, suggest improvements in our manners which we may profitably lay to heart.

In spite of his candor of speech, the red man displays a considerateness in some of his relations which is worthy of the white man's attention. Life in a tepee presents sundry phases which we who are accustomed to roomy houses would find difficult. The occupants are huddled together all the time in a small space, with no opportunity for retirement and self-communion. Not only must they avoid quarreling, but every one must respect the preference of every other to be alone now and then. The desired isolation is accomplished by a sign from the person who wishes to seclude himself, to which the family respond by absolutely ignoring his presence in the midst of them, and with such delicacy that it is as if he had suddenly become invisible. This continues till he gives a counter-sign, after which he is drawn once more into the common current. Self-effacement, with complete absorption in one's own meditations in disregard of the activities of all around one, is an art in which the Indians of the old order were trained, just as our youth are taught to commit their lessons to memory in a buzzing schoolroom, or to work intelligently in a shop where rattling machinery is in full motion on every side.

Then, there is the Indian's liking for the simple life. It would not be wise, probably, for us to carry our emulation of it into such details as his dietary and his style of habitation; but we can, with good effect, cultivate its spirit and enjoy its atmosphere. We can pass as much of our time as possible in the open air, including the sleeping hours; we can spread our tables with plain and healthful foods instead of heaping them with goads for the palate; and we can surround ourselves in our homes with only the things we really want, dismissing the worry of caring for a thousand things that we would rather be without, but with which we feel obliged to load ourselves because our neighbors have them.

With his patience and his indifference to hardship the red man has often surprised me. When we see him relinquishing a white man's job at which he has been receiving good wages, because he wishes to attend a tribal festival, we are too ready to conclude that he is vagrant-minded, fickle, unsteady. But when we watch him on a hunt in his own wilds, following the half-obliterated tracks of an elk over rolling country, or trailing a fugitive criminal through mountain labyrinths, we realize that such criticism is unjustly sweeping. Indian blanket-weavers, basketmakers, potters, silversmiths, all delve at their trades with a persistence which would do credit to artisans of any blood, and often their products represent not only long-continued toil, but a brave struggle with natural obstacles.

A few years ago I made a flying visit to an Indian station in the heart of Arizona, on my way to meet a Superintendent at a point perhaps seventy miles to the northward, measured in a bee-line across a practically trackless desert. To my dismay I found awaiting me a letter from the Superintendent proposing a change of plan, and making it necessary for me to communicate with him before nine o'clock the next morning. There was no telegraph line which could carry him a message, and the mail would take three or four days on account of the circuitous route it would have to travel. Evening was approaching. I sent for a Navajo Indian who was reputed an intelligent fellow, and who knew enough English to understand me without an interpreter. Upon him I impressed vigorously the importance of my business, and handed him a written communication which he was to deliver to the Superintendent before the sun had risen to a specified point in the heavens. It was like giving Lieutenant Rowan the message to Garcia: my Navajo made no comments and asked no ques-

tions, but went to his hogan for his wife, a little sack
of provender, and two ponies. I afterward learned
from the Superintendent that my note was delivered
to him at breakfast on the morning after it was written. I never saw my messenger again to get the
story of his night ride; but probably my readers will
agree with me that there is nothing slothful about
a man of any race who will perform an errand like
that as if it were a mere matter of course.

When we come to the domain of æsthetics, the Indian can give us a broad hint. It is true that he paints
his face and crowns his head with feathers, and wears
bead necklaces and gorgeous blankets—a scheme of
adornment which, in spite of his clever knack of com-
bining colors, bears the stamp of barbarism and subjects him to the ridicule of superficial critics; but at
least his costumes have the merit of individuality.
Our people dress as if they were all cut out of the
same piece. The long-tail coat may suit one man's
appearance and make another hideous; yet if the long
coat is decreed by fashion, both wear it. Although
our women allow themselves more latitude in minor
details, they, too, in the main, make a fetish of con-
formity. The world might not be any better place,
but certainly it would be a prettier one, if every human being wore that which best became him or represented his individual taste, instead of striving to escape
as far as possible from the exercise of any independent private judgment in attire.

Now, what have we to teach the red man? And
how?

The late Bishop Hare once said to me that if he

had the appointment of responsible field functionaries in the Indian Service, and were compelled to choose between a man who was dishonest in handling government property but clean and scrupulous in his home, and one who was straight in business matters but loose in his private morals, he would prefer the former to the latter. The government, the Bishop thought, could endure the loss of its money better than the Indians could afford to have a vicious example set them by a custodian to whom they looked for guidance. Fortunately, we are not reduced to such an alternative in recruiting the Indian Service. At the time the Bishop spoke, the Service was largely in the hands of professional politicians, not a few of whom drew a sharp line of distinction between their public and their domestic consciences; to-day it contains a small army of men who manage extensive interests without the misappropriation of a penny, and who are model husbands and fathers. It is to be regretted, however, that the isolation of their stations, and the lack of adequate schools near at hand, require that so many send their children away to be educated, at the very age when a child's part in the home life counts for something; and thus the Indians lose the advantage of an example of wholesome discipline among the young people in the families of their Superintendents and teachers.

Much effort will have to be expended on teaching the Indian the real meaning of some of the good gifts we are offering him. Like all primitive humankind, he finds it difficult to reason from the concrete to the abstract. He is keen enough in observing phenomena, but his mind, untrained in the art of working back from visible effects to their hidden causes, or forward to their remoter resultants, dismisses all these relations as enveloped in impenetrable mystery. Take the matter of education as an illustration. He sees white men everywhere setting a high value on it, and often willing to make great sacrifices to obtain it. Why? Because, one tells him, it adds vastly to the enjoyment of life. Another assures him that the educated man prospers better in a worldly way than the uneducated man. How, then, he inquires, can he get this education, which brings to others so much happiness and wealth? The school is pointed out to him as its dispenser. So the Indian who is too old to go to school himself is reconciled to sending his boy and girl. They acquire a smattering of several branches of knowledge, and then the adults of their tribe watch to see them enter upon lives of luxury. It does not occur to the minds of the watchers that the schooling is only the preparation of the intellectual soil, and that whatever grows out of it must come through an exercise of ingenuity and industry, and an assumption of responsibility, far more strenuous than anything found in the school. They have simply confounded symbol with substance.

The same is true of the religious ideal. That the Indian has religious concepts and leanings of his own, we have already noted. But religion, with him, deals so much with vagaries of divine favor and disfavor that often signs count for more than the realities behind them. Various ceremonial features of Christian worship, like kneeling or standing in prayer, bowing the head at certain signals, the passing of the sacramental bread and wine, the observance of fasts and feasts, assume in his thoughts, at the outset, an importance that casts their devotional meaning into shadow. I remember one prominent Indian who gave me a deal of trouble, in an investigation I was making, by his unblushing perjuries, but who was accustomed to boast of his habit of strict Sabbath-keeping. I knew another who, in his ambition to be recognized as a chief, did not hesitate to lead his fellow-tribesmen into falsehood, but in his formal loyalty to his church left nothing to be desired. In each instance, I think, the fault lay not so much in the man's conscious hypocrisy, as in an unfilled gap between the material and the figurative in his mind. Contrasting the religion of his fathers with that which he had adopted from the white man, he had regarded these rather as rival " medicines "—that is, as competitive devices for conciliating the divinities—than as expressions of two utterly dissimilar spiritual attitudes. The nobler view of the subject, let us hope, came later. The cases are mentioned here only to show one of the bridges across which the red man must be led by his white brother before he can stand on firm ground.

Here and there in Red Men's Land we come upon an extraordinary mixture of Christianity and paganism woven into a distinctive religion. Such was the ghost-dancing, or Messiah excitement, which broke out among the Indians on the great plains twenty-odd years ago. The leaders of the movement preached that the government of the world was on the eve of a new dispensation, which was to be ushered in by the advent of a Messiah, or messenger from the Great Spirit, one of whose functions it would be to restore to the Indians the dominion the whites had wrested from them, and bring the whole people back to the simple life which preceded the European invasion. The dancing which was a chief feature of the demonstration ended usually in trances, sometimes accompanied by convulsions and sometimes by a death-like rigidity of the body and a suspension of sensation. By degrees, some of the Indians who had been within reach of Christian instruction began to mingle a few Christian rites with the original manifestations of hysteria, and this gave the followers of the cult an excuse for meeting at intervals to pass a night in chanting, prayer, exhortation, and the consumption of peyote, a native drug which induces visions like those of opium or hasheesh.

Among the Indians on the northern Pacific slope we find a religion locally styled "Shakerism." Crosses and candles mounted on a white altar are its most conspicuous emblems; the ringing of dinner-bells furnishes its music; its active exercises run largely to dances in which the sexes face each other and advance and retreat as they sing, meanwhile shaking their hands and bodies to drive out their sins, and an individual dancer occasionally falls to the floor insensible. At their stated meetings the elect wear white robes, and cross themselves when they gravely exchange greetings. They have a sort of baptismal service which is repeated whenever they come together, with a phraseology obviously adapted from the baptismal and confirmation services of Christian churches. They perform also the apostolic rite of the laying-on of hands to heal the sick; but upon this they have grafted the pagan conceit of creating a tremendous din at the bedside of the patient in order to exorcise the demons that possess him. In justice to the ghost-dancers and the Indian " Shakers," I should add that those who are most earnest in their faith are, as a rule, a fairly law-abiding element.

The Caucasian ideal of citizenship is almost as hard for the Indian to comprehend as the Caucasian ideal of religion. All he sees of its obligations, at first, is the necessity of paying taxes, and of meeting his private engagements on their technical terms as the sole means of escaping a suit at law. These requirements fill him with terror, as he does not understand interest charges or penalties for deferred payments, but realizes that back of the tax-gatherer and the usurer stands the sheriff at the auction-block. Of the privileges of citizenship, two focus his attention: he can vote and hold office, and, if so inclined, can buy and drink whiskey as freely as the white man. His vote, too commonly, he values more for the uses to which he can put it for his personal profit in one way or another, than for its broader import, or possible public service. Here is where we have still before us a very large task in training the Indian for his new civic affiliations.

I hope I shall not be misinterpreted when I say that among the other lessons we shall have to teach the Indian is that of an enlightened selfishness. It will sound like the paradox of " being cruel in order

to be kind," when I explain that an impulse of selfishness is an essential ingredient of all true generosity.
The child who cares nothing for his toys does not
mind parting with them; when we undertake to cultivate in him a sense of the beauty of giving, we encourage him to sacrifice some object which he really prizes
in order to give pleasure to some one else. Most
normal children need no preliminary training in selfishness: they absorb its spirit from their social atmosphere. But the Indian who has learned from childhood to magnify the glory of giving, not that the
beneficiary may be happier but that the giver may
have praises heaped upon him in the presence of the
multitude, presents a serious problem; and we puzzle
him sorely with the inconsistency of our philosophy
of life when with one breath we insist on his holding
fast to his own, and with the next advise him to give
away as much as he can spare, and in a manner which
will bring him no visible benefit.

The trouble is that what passes with the Indian
for generosity is not generosity at all, but mere prodigality. The falseness of the aboriginal standard is
revealed when a man ambitious for fame as a giver
has stripped himself of most that he owns, and then
falls back upon others to feed and clothe him. This
is a wrong to those who have been more provident.
The government and the missionaries have had a long,
hard struggle in their effort to break up the practice
of gift-dances, where the host of the occasion spreads
a public feast, and scatters among his guests his blankets, his guns, his ponies, his pipes, his household
utensils—in short, whatever of his property any one

present may covet—for no better reason than that
such unrestrained largess is, according to the traditions of his people, a royal road to eminence. When
Indians were first allowed to sell lands which had come
to them by inheritance, many of the sellers, even those
who had not for years had a penny of their own to
spend, squandered their money at once on all sorts
of follies, and on gifts which they distributed among
friends and strangers indiscriminately. Then, having within a few hours risen from penury to affluence
and sunk to penury again, they fell back for support
upon any relatives who could be reached, and led a
life of pauperism to the end, or till another windfall
came their way. The relatives thus victimized, little
as they enjoyed the experience, repressed any impulse
to rebel, because that would have exposed them to a
charge of stinginess, the meanest offense recognized
in the red man's code.

Of course, no people encumbered with such standards can hope to keep step with modern progress. It
therefore becomes an important part of our business
to teach the red man to husband his resources and cling
to them as his right, loosening his hold only in response
to the appeal of a worthy object, and then giving
not merely without thought of advantage to himself,
but with due foresight, so that his liberality shall be
at his own expense and not at that of his kinsfolk.
More than once, intelligent Indians have protested to
me against a grant of citizenship to a certain member
of their tribe, on the ground that he would undoubtedly sell his allotment as soon as he was free to do
so, throw the proceeds away recklessly, and saddle

himself for the rest of his life upon some branch of
his family who were already having all they could
do to get along.

It is common to ascribe the origin of every form
of self-indulgence among the Indians to white influence. The white race surely has enough to answer
for, but it did not teach the red race to befog its brains
with strong drink, or to smoke, or to gamble. Tobacco was found in use among these people by the
earliest explorers; and various ferments made of
grasses and roots, of the bark of the pine tree, and
of berry juices, mashed maize treated with water and
wood ashes, and a liquid expressed from the fruit of
the giant cactus, afforded aboriginal tipplers the means
of satisfying their craving for stimulants. As for
games of chance, the Indian had many before he ever
saw a playing-card, and some of those which are most
characteristic appear to have descended to him from
a prehistoric era. What the white man has done in
these lines is to make it easier for the Indian to become a drunkard, to encourage him to be a worse one,
and to give a more serious turn to his gambling by
introducing a mercenary motive into what began as a
simple and good-humored amusement.

With the gambling practice the government has been
practically unable to cope. It can be carried on in
secret; the worsted parties never complain of the vic-
tors; and none of the gamesters bear on their persons
any mark of their indulgence. Intoxication, on the
other hand, is a sufficient proof that strong drink is
now, or has very recently been, near at hand, and this
affords the constabulary at least a point of departure

in their search for contraband liquors. The federal
statutes have always been very strict in their prohibition of the introduction of intoxicants into the Indian
country, and of selling or giving them to any Indian
ward of the government anywhere in the United
States; but until the second year of my administration as Commissioner Congress had not appropriated
any fund worth mentioning to pay the expenses of
an organized effort to suppress the traffic. Then it
placed $25,000 at my disposal for this purpose.

With the aid of one of the great temperance societies I was able to secure the services of William E.
Johnson, who had already a notable record as a cam-
paigner, and who combined the shrewdness of a de-
tective and the courage of a soldier with a gift for
infusing his own enthusiasm into his subordinates.
The plans he projected required a large appropriation,
and, in view of the mettle he displayed in his first
year's work, Congress was not slow to vote the money;
the annual grant jumped suddenly to $40,000, and
was carried up by degrees till it reached $80,000 in the
last year of his service. He kept a brigade of men
and women scattered all over the Indian country, continually at work ferreting out the dealers who supplied Indians with liquor, and his descents upon the
offenders were so noiseless and so sure that he acquired the nickname of " Pussyfoot." He was a terror to wrongdoers in his special field, and his resigna-
tion in 1911 was one of the severest losses the Indian
Bureau has ever sustained, though the pace he set
has remained a tradition for the inspiration of his
successors.

We have seen that the Indian is not wasteful by deliberate intent; his shortcomings in this regard are due to ignorance, or his different point of view. He seems to us wasteful of space, because the great areas over which his people have always roamed have had no value in their eyes except as a game preserve, a source of fuel and water, and a grazing ground for their horses or cattle. Even what has been used for tillage has been only a trifling plot here and there. In Red Man's Land, such a thing as agriculture in the broader sense is confined almost wholly to the white settlers, and the intensive culture on which posterity must pin its hopes is hardly known yet to the whites. Time is another element which, in our busy life, we reckon at a definite valuation, but which to the Indian seems worthless. Just as we must teach him that an acre of land means, with the right labor expended on it, the feeding of so many human beings, so we must make him understand that a day or an hour frittered away, or not counted in the cost of any undertaking, is so much provision for the future wasted. In other words, it must be impressed upon him that the hand-to-mouth, happy-go-lucky mode of existence, which answered for his fathers, will no longer protect him from suffering, and still less his children.

Comfort, convenience, expedients for labor-saving, and the distinction between morality and decency are among the other things of which the red man has but the vaguest notion. His tepee or cabin is warmed only fitfully and ventilated only by accident. The idea of so equipping his dwelling that the heat shall enter it regularly through one aperture while the vitiated air is carried off through another, and that these processes shall go on independently of the whims of the wind outside, does not suggest itself to his mind till some instructor lays hold of his education in the modern arts of living. It is only within recent years that any of the Pueblo Indians, though building houses of stone and adobe, have crowned these with chimneys; and for a good while after they had been induced to try chimneys, many, assuming that whatever virtue there might be in such structures was due to some magical charm, neglected to connect them with the fireplaces. I have seen an Indian camp pitched within a mile of a fine spring, and the women trudging the whole distance two or three times a day, carrying heavy clay water-pots on their heads, because it had not struck any of the party as worth while to move the camp nearer to the source of supply. We despise the shiftless white man who is content to " get along somehow " in order to save himself a little trouble; the Indian, left to himself, " gets along somehow " because he does not know how to do anything better.

Akin to this ignorance is his false sense of proportion, and the childish stubbornness he sometimes manifests when his guardians have most conscientiously warned him, in terms that he can and does comprehend, of the short-sightedness of a certain course to which he is committing himself. For example, I was appealed to once to procure new allotments of land for a considerable group of Indians well past middle age. As young men, the government had allotted them each a homestead in the midst of a thrifty farming country.   According to the letter of the law authorizing their allotments, every member of the tribe was to be allowed to decide for himself where he would take his land.   This particular band chose theirs on a wooded hillside, where the soil was poor and the grass sparse, but where shade was abundant and the view fine.   In vain the allotting agent strove to win them away from this choice by showing them how hopeless a task it would be to try to raise crops there, and how the country around them would fill up presently so that they could not move no matter how bitterly they might repent their blunder.   They contemptuously retorted that they knew what they wanted better than any white man could tell them. Was not this a place where they could lie under the trees and sweep the neighboring landscape with their eyes?   And would not these same groves furnish them with fuel through the long winters?

So there they settled, and stayed till the agent's forebodings were fulfilled.   The region did become thickly populated, and all the farming lands were taken up by wiser men; meanwhile, their beautiful groves retreated before the axe, as blazing hearths demanded the sacrifice of tree after tree, and neighbors tempted them with offers of money for lumber and cordwood.   And bye-and-bye the foolish little colony found themselves high and dry on their bare hillside with nothing to eat and no soil which they could cultivate for food.   It was a sad plight, but one which could not be remedied without robbing the less obstinate tribesmen who, under the allotting agent's advice, had preferred arable acres to shade and scenery.

The relation between morality and decency is one which usually puzzles the Indian, and which, I am bound to confess, seems too subtle for many of our own race who have enjoyed more advantages. I have seen adult Indians going about, in the midst of a mixed company of whites, wearing garments so full of holes and gaps as to be little better than none at all, yet honestly unconscious of offence. I have known an old chief to walk into the house of a white friend, and, meeting no one on the lower floor, to ascend the stairs and penetrate the room of one of the ladies of the family without knocking; yet when he was peremptorily ordered out, he was astonished and grieved, so unsuspicious was he that he had been doing anything reprehensible. There were no stairs in his tepee, no locks on its flap, no partitions inside, no barriers of any sort to the coming and going of whomsoever would, though it was occupied by all the members of his household and their guests; and it had never occurred to him that, so long as he cherished no unfriendly design, he had been guilty of wrong or even impoliteness in thus intruding. I have Indian friends who are personally as respectable, and, according to their lights, as pure-minded, as the white class to which I belong, who do not hesitate to discuss the innermost privacies of life in general conversation, and with the same freedom with which we might talk about the weather. Here is, plainly, a difference between the social codes of the primitive and the sophisticated man, in matters of appearance, without regard to any evil motive in the background. If we would have the Indian escape much damaging misjudgment in dealing with his white neighbors, we must teach him to respect their best-intrenched conventions and observe the essentials of their scheme of morality.

Finally, we must teach the Indian the virtue—the necessity, in fact—of self-dependence in the new order of life which we are opening before him. His reliance on " government " for everything he wants from food and raiment, medical attendance and education, down to legal aid in his private litigation, must cease. It has been absorbed by him from the paternalism with which we have saturated our management of his affairs. A few of the tribes have always been too proud to yield to this enervating influence, and have insisted in a manly spirit on their right to take care of themselves without assistance from Washington, but most of them have become more or less demoralized, and it is only recently that some of the rising generation have taken the back track of their own volition. They have organized a Society of American Indians—let the name be noted, for it has no connection with any other Indian society or order —which is making excellent headway. It is composed of some of the most enterprising and honorably ambitious young persons of both sexes in the several tribes, and includes in its associate membership a number of white friends and advisers who have no selfish interest to serve. It promises to be very useful to the red people everywhere by pointing a way for their redemption from their present state of dependence, and assuring their larger participation in the work of fitting themselves for citizenship.

Here, in closing, let me remind the reader of what I said at the outset of this volume—that I should deal only with generalities. I have held strictly to this line, leaving out of special consideration the little handful of Indians found in every tribe who have apprehended the meaning and adopted the standards of the higher civilization. My aim has been to show what difficulties confront us in our effort to lead, not the well-qualified few, but the great ignorant mass of the dwellers in Red Man's Land, from their ancient into our modern environment, from the age of stone into the age of steel, out of the shadows of a barbarism swarming with myths and mysteries into the sunlight of a culture rooted in eternal truth.

MISSIONS TO THE RED MAN

IN the preceding pages we read that when our government found it necessary to recognize the scattered tribes of primitive savages in different parts of our unsurveyed territory, it began by dealing with them as foreign nations. Treaties were made which the tribes could not read and could but imperfectly comprehend. Reservations were set off and the Indians were shut in. Laws were framed for them—by those who knew little or nothing of Indian life and traditions—to control them and to compel them to remain within certain limits. Agencies were established far removed from civilization and beyond observation—often beyond investigation. Agents with no knowledge of Indian nature or its ingrained characteristics, even when they were just in purpose, were naturally without the sympathy requisite to gain the confidence and good-will of those who resented the encroachments upon their traditional rights.

Not understanding and not understood, and otherwise helpless, these untamed races met the civilization of force with the force of their barbarism. The natural results were the frequent bloody outbreaks and the Indian wars in one tribe or another since the white man took possession of the country. To subdue the Indians, government money was poured out like water. Indians were slaughtered and white men were slaughtered, and nothing was gained except resentful submission to force.

While this was the national method—we can hardly call it policy—there were those who from the very beginning believed in "a more excellent way." There is a power greater than that of armies—the power which can change the hearts and lives of men, even those called savages, and make them friends; this they knew. They knew that subjugation is a far cry from civilization, and that Christianity alone has the secret of life which carries with it all the motives and conditions of a true and permanent civilization. When the inner life is reached and renewed, then is that saying true, " Behold, I make all things new."

Acting upon the personal experience of this " power of God " to change the dispositions and the will of man, came the beginnings of missionary history among the Indians in the early settlement of our country. Roger Williams was the pioneer evangelical missionary to the primitive red men. While yet in England he had advocated the colonization of the New World for the propagation of the gospel to the Indians, and soon after his arrival he applied himself to their evangelization. He wrote: " God was pleased to give me a patient spirit to lodge with them in their filthy, smoky holes, even while I lived in Plymouth and Salem, to gain their tongue." He preached to the Pequots, Narragansetts and other tribes in Rhode Island, as he says, " to their great delight and convictions."

DENOMINATIONAL MISSIONS
BAPTIST

The first organized effort of the Baptists for the evangelization of the Indians was coincident with the opening of the Nineteenth Century. In 1801, Baptist missionaries labored among the Tuscaroras and other tribes of Western New York. In 1817, the work extended among the Cherokees, the Miamis and Kickapoos, and in Michigan among the Potawatomies and Ottawas; in 1828, among the Ojibwas. Next came missions in Georgia among the Creeks; the Otowes and Omahas in 1822, and the Delawares and Stockbridges in 1833. As far back as 1857 there were reported 1,320 Baptist church members in Indian Territory. From the first mission onward consecrated missionaries have wrought with great fidelity and patience; if often with little encouragement, yet at length with rich rewards in the transformed character and lives of those whom they found barbarians.

Missionary work with the Kiowas, begun in 1904, is now gladdened with fifteen Baptist churches, with 1,011 church members—including the Apache, Hopi, Navajo and Crow tribes, among whom flourishing missions exist, as among the Monas of California. Among the Cheyennes and Arapahoes missions began in 1895; there are now four churches, with 266 communicants. In Western Oklahoma ten churches rejoice in 958 members; and to-day in two tribes and in Oklahoma there are about 4,500 Indians who are members of Baptist churches. Many of these are ministered to by native preachers, some of whom have much ability. Indian University at Muskogee, Okla., ministers largely to civilized tribes. The denomination has expended among the Indians over $400,000. The average annual expenditure is about $20,000.

Many of the chiefs and leading men in the various tribes have been converted. These have wrought for the peace of the land as the government could not do, and have done much to lay the foundations for the future of a peace that shall express itself in Christian brotherhood.

CONGREGATIONAL

In 1646, Eliot and Mayhew were "apostles" to the Indians. Eliot wrote: "I found a pregnant-witted young Indian who had been a servant in an English house, who pretty well understood our language, and well understood his own. By his help I translated the Commandments and many texts of Scripture." The more purely personal work of these missionaries and of Sargent and Wheelock among the New England tribes was followed by no organized work by the Congregationalists until 1815, when the American Board for Foreign Missions began its missions. At that time the entire Indian population of the country was estimated to be 240,000. Soon missions were established among the Cherokees, Chickasaws and Creeks, and later, in 1827, the work was more widely extended. The difficulties of the missionaries were greatly increased by the frequent violations of the government treaties. The mission among the Cherokees was broken up by the State of Georgia—a black page of history. This led to missions in the Northwest, fifteen in all, especial attention being given to the 40,000 Sioux. These warlike tribes were subject to great exasperations by the constant encroachments of unscrupulous white men, which hindered and imperilled Christian efforts. In 1847, the American Missionary Association began missions among the Chippewas, the Ojibwas and

Ottawas in Michigan, and, as the year passed, in Wisconsin and Washington territories. The American Board at Santee, Nebr., after ten years among the Sioux, had organized and maintained a church of more than 200 converted Indians, which was in the care of a native pastor of exceptional ability and Christian devotion. In 1882, the entire organized missionary work of the Congregational churches among the Indians came under the care of the American Missionary Association, and since that time there has been significant advance both in the development of schools for Christian education and for evangelization in the Indian encampments. Twenty-one Indian churches, with 114 missionaries and more than 11,000 church members, are taking the Light of the world into the darkness of paganism.

FRIENDS

The Friends' Missions began in 1870, when President Grant apportioned the care of the Indians among the different religious denominations. There are now ten stations with resident missionaries among the Shawnees, the Osages, Modocs and Kickapoos in Oklahoma. The earlier years of the Friends' work were largely devoted to education, but since the government schools have come to care for the secular education the missions have confined themselves to direct evangelization to Christianize the Indians. During the past year twelve Indians have been hopefully converted and have entered upon Christian life. A steady advance has been apparent among many of the Indians, and the scale of general intelligence perceptibly improves, accompanied in many cases by improvement in morals. The Friends are withdrawing from stations where Indians and whites are living in the same communities, to give more attention to strictly Indian work among uncivilized tribes. The appropriation for the year was $5,577.

METHODIST EPISCOPAL

The Indian missions of the Methodist Episcopal Church (including those of the Woman's Home Missionary Society) are located in Washington, Oregon, Arizona, Wisconsin, Minnesota, Montana, Nevada, California, New

Mexico, North Carolina, Michigan, Kansas and Oklahoma. In twenty-four tribes and other parts of tribes there are forty Indian churches and twenty-one Indian stations, in which twenty-two white and ten Indian missionaries are engaged. These churches report 2,300 members, with 5,000 adherents, who hear the gospel and are hopeful subjects for missionary endeavor; all maintain Sunday-schools, with an enrolment of 1,600 children. The Woman's Society has an industrial home and school for the Navajos at Farmington, N. M.; settlement work in Washington, and mission stations in California, Kansas and Oklahoma. The total appropriation for the year is $21,502.

METHODIST EPISCOPAL CHURCH, SOUTH

The Methodist Episcopal Church, South, numbers 2,900 Indian communicants in Oklahoma, with twenty-five Indian ministers, who labor there among four tribes.

The Woman's Missionary Council employs a missionary among the Kiowas; she visits in the camps, teaches the Bible and holds mothers' meetings.

MORAVIAN

The evangelization of the Indians was one of the chief motives which brought the Moravians to America. The work began in 1735. It was unpopular from the start with the white settlers, as also with some of the Indian tribes. The early missionaries pursued their work in Georgia, North Carolina, New York, Pennsylvania and Connecticut. As their charges were forced westward, the missionaries accompanied them. Zeizsberger, the greatest, who served more years with the Indians than any other missionary, not excepting Eliot, was adopted by the warlike Iroquois and made their archivist, and for one whole year (1777-78) prevented them from attacking the exposed western frontier of the American colonies during the Revolution—a fact little known.

The missions suffered persecutions, and even frightful massacres, at the hands of the whites, completely destroying some stations. As the red men moved, the work was carried into Ohio, Illinois, Michigan, Ontario, Indian Territory and Kansas, but all stations have now been given up or handed over to other denominations, except five in California, manned by three ordained clergymen and their wives, ministering definitely to about 300 souls, besides a large number of adherents. The salary of one of the missionary couples is paid by a group of twenty young people's societies in the East. The board expends from $2,000 to $3,000 per annum.

PRESBYTERIAN

Presbyterian missions for the Indian date back to a long line of self-sacrificing missionaries among the Cherokees, Chippewas, Choctaws, Sioux, Umatillas and Nez Percés down to the present-day company of devoted men and women, faithful witnesses to the grace and power of the gospel of Christ. The missions of the Presbyterian Church are large with results and have abundantly justified the faith of those who have sustained them in the long series of years. The work at the present time is in twenty-six states, among fifty-seven tribal divisions. There are one hundred and thirty-four missionaries now under appointment of the Presbyterian Board of Missions, eighteen of whom are entirely supported by Indian churches and native missionary societies. There are one hundred and sixteen organized churches, with one hundred and eighteen additional stations, where services are held under the ministry of thirty-nine Indian missionaries. These Indian churches number more than 7,000 communicants and more than 18,000 adherents, who to a greater or less extent are receptive of the influences of the gospel. Eleven mission schools are educating and training 473 pupils.

These Presbyterian missions are located in California, Oregon, Washington, Idaho, Utah, Wyoming, North and South Dakota, Montana, Wisconsin, Michigan, Nebraska, Kansas, Oklahoma, Colorado, New Mexico, Arizona and also among the Iroquois in the State of New York—a great record. Much interest is felt in Indian missions in Alaska. The missions among the Sioux in South Dakota have been blessed with exceptional results, the Yankton Indians being especially noted for their development in education and in Christian character, and for their progress in the knowledge and practice of civilized life.

PROTESTANT EPISCOPAL

Indian missions of the Protestant Episcopal Church began in Colonial days. In 1701 a missionary was sent to the Six Nations living in the valley of the Mohawk. After the Revolutionary War, which interrupted all missionary work, this church renewed its interest, and from that day until now has been most zealous and constant in its ministering, with large rewards in Christian conversions and the development of Christian character and life.

To-day its Domestic and Foreign Missionary Society is carrying on hopeful work for the Indians in Alaska, Arizona, Minnesota, Wisconsin, Idaho, Oklahoma, California, Utah, Wyoming, South Dakota and Florida. Recent Indian missions in Alaska have been greatly blessed. Its greatest work has been in South Dakota where ninety-five stations in charge of twenty-three clergy—of whom sixteen are Indians—are ministering to 11,705 Sioux, of whom 4,982 are communicants of the church. The gifts of these communicants alone to the Episcopal Church amount to more than $10,000 year by year. This fact speaks for itself.

The entire work of the missions requires the services of forty-eight clergymen, one hundred and fifteen laymen and fifty-one women, who minister to 6,000 Indian communicants scattered over twelve dioceses and districts, with a yearly expenditure of no less than $76,028. Wherever this church has planted itself by church, chapel and schools, there has been a gratifying advance in morals and manner of living.

REFORMED CHURCH IN AMERICA

The Indian missions of the Reformed Church in America are efficiently directed and administered by the Women's Board of Domestic Missions. They are carried on among the Arapahoes, Cheyennes, Apaches, Comanches in Oklahoma, the Winnebagos in Nebraska and the Mescaleros in New Mexico. These various missions call for the ministry of eighteen missionaries and four interpreters.

Among the Arapahoes and Cheyennes there is a church membership of 273 Christian Indians, with 130 youths enrolled in the Sunday-schools. The native Christians in this comparatively recent missionary work contributed during the past year for Christian missions and evangelization among their people the sum of $534.58.

In April last the Fort Sill Apaches, who were held by the government as prisoners-of-war, were released and the tribe was broken up. One hundred and seventy-five were transferred to the Mescalero Reservation, among the mountains of New Mexico, where a band of Apaches had for some time been located. A part of the tribe elected to remain in Oklahoma. A ministry among them has been continued. Of this warlike Apache tribe thirty-one were received into the communion of the church last year. In the Comanche Mission eighteen have been received in church membership during the past year, and there has been a beautiful response to Christian influences.

In the Mescalero Apache Mission seventeen, during the year 1913, united with the church on confession of their faith in Christ. To this church were added by letter on one Sunday eighty-eight of the Apache members transferred from Fort Sill.

The work among the Winnebagos, begun five years ago, has been wonderfully successful. There are 200 members of the church, all of whom have been won in this short time. The work has been made more difficult through the vices of white people. The suppression of the liquor traffic among the Indians has met with strong opposition, but the Christian influence has been yet stronger and the work is hopeful under God's favor.

There are in all 750 Indians in the communion of the Reformed Church in America in connection with its missions.

The total amount expended for the year in these several missions was $27,152.

UNDENOMINATIONAL MISSIONS

The National Indian Rights Association has Indian missions in Arizona, Wisconsin, California and New Mexico. This association does pioneer work and has planted fifty missions which have been transferred to other hands.

Y. M. C. A. AND Y. W. C. A.

The Young Men's and the Young Women's Christian Associations have engaged in a specially important feature of missionary work among the pupils in the various government schools and among the returned students on the Indian reservations These students, on returning from schools such as Carlisle and Hampton to the comparative isolation and limitations of tribal life, are not only subject to temptations incident to both heredity and environment, but they also greatly feel the differences in the changes and modes of life. These two associations come to them when they realize the need of friendly sympathy and friendly hands extended in Christian love and brotherhood and sisterhood. The young Indian people—35,000 being returned students—are very happy to be included in organizations which take in students of the wide world, and it is a great inspiration and motive for them that they may be thus associated. These Young Men's Christian Associations and Young Women's Christian Associations have proved to be greatly helpful in thus ministering to those who are likely to be of future influence in their tribes, and they should be generously encouraged in their interesting work.

UNTILLED FIELDS

Meanwhile, the fact faces the churches that there are 54,000 Indians among whom no missionary work is being conducted, and that 24,000 Indian children of school age have no school facilities and are not in any school. This may assure the Christian people of our country that the red man needs all of these missions, and needs them greatly.

GOVERNMENT EDUCATION AND MISSIONS

When in 1870 a new Indian policy was inaugurated by the United States Government, it was really a by-product of the various Christian missions. The missions had taught the government a lesson. It had come to realize that the red man could indeed take on civilization, and that patient missionary fidelity and devotion were assuredly transforming character and life. Hence, came the system of education in government schools as a preparation for Indian manhood and citizenship. Since that time the government has expended about $350,000,-000 in the development of its Indian policy, including education, which has brought a new day for the Indian. The government must have credit for the lesson it learned, though it took a long time to learn it. It could, however, but in part adopt the missionary idea. It could give the Indian secular education; but it could offer nothing to meet the Indians' most immediate and supremest need.

The red man has an instinct for religion. He has always believed in the Infinite Spirit. His untutored heart asked after God. But we are not left in ignorance as to what his religion was. It exists to-day. It was and is the religion of darkened minds and darkened hearts, swarming with myths and mysteries, and the rankest superstitions, the fruitage of which could be nothing other than the gross heathenism which missionaries have found in all tribes and which still exists among the tribes uninfluenced by Christianity, and so far as tribes have not yielded to this influence.·

The government in its new policy, with its secular schools, had no religion to offer the Indian. It could educate, but it could not evangelize, convert and nurture him in the Christian faith. It could not provide for his spiritual nature. That is not the function of the government. It is not engaged in regenerating the inner life of its subjects. Yet without this renewal in the spirit of his mind the red man can never be redeemed from heathenism and fitted for life, with standards and character that will meet the tests of life here and hereafter. The missions went to the Indians with the promise of a gracious life, and they made it good. The gospel of Jesus Christ does change the red man's ideas and ideals of life. It does renew the spirit of his mind. He becomes a new man in his affections and desires. The missions have brought and do bring the bread of life to the hunger of his heart.

The marks of a progress that is steady and full of hopeful purpose are all along in the paths of the missionaries. " The Christian Indian," says Dr. Riggs, who has spent his entire life among the Sioux, "is the only man among them all who in the movement toward civilization keeps his place and holds fast to the progress he has made."

In the limitations of this chapter it is not possible to illustrate by special examples the appeal which Christian missions make for the Indian. Allow one—from a missionary product, David Hare, a Sioux:—"What we need is a Christian education that will strengthen us to resist the adversaries which come with the White Man's civilization. The government is doing much for our people, and must be given credit for what it has accomplished, but it is Christianity that changes the people. The real salvation must be from the inside, and not from the outside. All the forces at work for the government for our advancement do not and could not come up to the work which the patient, earnest missionary is doing and has done from the beginning."

A like word comes from Henry Roe Cloud, a Winnebago, brought to know and follow Christ by a missionary, a graduate of Yale University in the class of 1910. "It is very important," he says, "to remember that the salvation of the Indian must be from within. I should not be true to the deepest convictions of my soul if I did not say this. Now is the time to go after the Indian and to strengthen by the power of the gospel the work of these missions."

These men are types. One whose life has been devoted to the red man brings the final word. It is this: "Through our Christian missions there is a change in thought and in outlook of far more importance than all others, for it marks the growth of manhood and gives permanent hope for the future. The spirit of Christianity has greatly changed the Indians' thought. We have taught them that Christ came to save men from evil; that religion is more than an outward change; that it means a change of heart which will insure all right development. This and this only will bring a wild and insubordinate race of people to become gentle, kind, thoughtful and industrious. And in this teaching we have not failed."

MISSIONS IN ALASKA

The Congregational Home Missionary Society and the American Missionary Association have been working in Alaska among the Eskimos and others for more than twenty years. They have a church of Eskimos in Northern Alaska, on Bering Strait, of more than three hundred members.

The Board of Missions of the Protestant Episcopal Church has a large and very important work in Alaska, among the Eskimos, the Indians and the miners and traders. Work is sustained at twenty-five localities. Fairbanks, the metropolis of central Alaska, was a new mining plant when Bishop Rowe secured an early entrance for the church. The log building which was a chapel on Sundays, became a reading room on week-days for the rough-clad miners. A hospital was built which ministered to the sick through a wide range of territory. Missions both to white men and Indians have spread along the valley of the river on either hand, and now Fairbanks is the center of what is known as the Tanana Valley Mission, with half a score of workers, schools and missions, hospitals and reading rooms, and carrying everywhere the message of the Master.

At Fort Yukon, far up the great river, is a missionary physician, the only one within five hundred miles of his post, and the dauntless doctor with his dog team counts one hundred and fifty miles as nothing in an effort to minister to the suffering.

In addition to its work for white populations in Alaska, the Presbyterian Church has now eleven missions for native Alaskans, with thirty-two outstations. Ten of these missions (Wrangell, Sitka, Juneau, Haines, Hoonah, Klawock, Klukwan, Saxman, Hydaburg, and Kake) are in the southeast or Sitkan peninsula. One missionary is at Barrow, the northernmost point of Alaska.

Under the Woman's Board of Home Missions, the school work is now centralized at the Sheldon Jackson School (in Sitka), newly built and equipped, a co-educational boarding school for Alaskan youth of all tribes. The course of study, in which Bible instruction is emphasized, covers eight grades. Vocational training includes domestic science, domestic art, wood-carving, carpentry, blacksmith work, boat-building, etc.

At Haines, there is a small hospital in charge of a physician and two helpers, treating three hundred and fifty patients a month.

Under the Board of Home Missions are seven ordained missionaries for native work, with five who minister also to white parishioners. There are eleven native helpers. The Woman's Board supports the three workers at Haines, and the fifteen at Sheldon Jackson School.

During the fiscal year 1912-13, the Board of Home Missions, including the Woman's Board, expended $50,222 for native work in Alaska.

The Methodist Episcopal Church supports missionaries in Alaska, at Fairbanks, Juneau, Ketchikan, Nome, Seward, and Skagway. The Woman's Home Missionary Society has an industrial home and school, with a hospital, on Unalaska, one of the islands of the Aleutian chain. This ministers to the needs of Aleuts, while Eskimo on the mainland are reached through mission stations at Nome and Sinuk. Total appropriation of the church for current year, for Alaskan work, $19,654.

BIBLIOGRAPHY

(Order books from the publishers named, *not* from denominational headquarters.)

D. Appleton & Co.
The Story of the Indian. George Bird Grinnell. $1.50.

Doubleday, Page & Co.
The Vanishing Race. Dr. Joseph Dixon. $3.50
Indian Boyhood. Charles Eastman. $1.60.

Duffield & Co.
The Indian of To-day. George Bird Grinnell. $2.00.
Geronimo's Story of His Life. $1.50.

Houghton Mifflin Company.
The Soul of the Indian. Charles Eastman. $1.00.

Indian Department. Washington, D. C.
Indian Affairs: Laws and Treaties.

L. C. Page & Co.
Our Little Indian Cousin. Mary Hazelton Wade. $.60.

Little, Brown & Co.
The Indian Dispossessed. Seth K. Humphrey. $1.50.
The Oregon Trail. Francis Parkman. $1.50.

Macmillan Company.
Lights and Shadows of a Long Episcopate. Rt. Rev. H. B. Whipple. $2.00.

Presbyterian Board of Publications.
The Story of Marcus Whitman. $1.00.

Public Library.
The North American Indian. Edward S. Curtis. (20 vols.)
The Indian's Book. Natalie Curtis.
Indian Story and Song. Alice Fletcher.

Revell Company.
The Apostle of the North. James Evans. $1.25.
Two Wilderness Voyagers. F. W. Calkins. $.50.
My Host the Enemy. F. W. Calkins. $.50.
Life of Sheldon Jackson. Robert L. Stewart. $2.00.
Among the Thlingets. Livingstone F. Jones. $1.50.

Charles Scribner's Sons.
The Indian and His Problem. Francis E. Leupp. $2.00.
Missionary Explorers Among the American Indians. M. G. Humphreys. $1.50.